JAKE PARISH

The Leadership Edge

From Hiring to High-Performance Strategies to Attract, Retain, and Optimize Exceptional Leadership

Copyright © 2025 by Jake Parish

All rights reserved. No part of this publication may be reproduced, stored or transmitted in any form or by any means, electronic, mechanical, photocopying, recording, scanning, or otherwise without written permission from the publisher. It is illegal to copy this book, post it to a website, or distribute it by any other means without permission.

First edition

This book was professionally typeset on Reedsy.
Find out more at reedsy.com

Contents

Introduction: The Power of Exceptional Leadership, My...   iv

1   Who This Book Is For: Understanding the Challenges Faced by...   1

2   About the Author: My Experience, Expertise, and Lessons in...   12

3   The Value You'll Gain from this book   21

4   The Innovex Approach: From Discovery to Placement,...   37

5   Key Leadership Challenges: Identifying the Right Talent,...   52

6   Frameworks and Strategies for Success: Building High-Impact...   71

7   Practical Strategies for Retaining Top Talent Through...   84

8   Real-World Case Studies: Lessons in Leadership...   100

9   Taking Action: Steps, Tools & Templates for Leadership...   124

Final Thoughts   149

Introduction: The Power of Exceptional Leadership, My Executive Search Journey, and the Purpose of This Book

Leadership is the compass that guides an organization through the complexities of growth, change, and competition. No organization succeeds without true leadership. Regardless of the amazing talents and professionals in an organization, exceptional leadership is needed to harness and strategically organize these talents and professionals to achieve the stated organizational goals.

At Innovex, a leader is as defined as a highly skilled and emotionally intelligent professional. Exceptional leadership goes beyond merely assigning tasks and ensuring compliance with organizational policies. It serves as the driving force that aligns vision with execution, propels teams toward innovation, and builds a thriving workplace culture.

As leadership expert John C. Maxwell puts it, "A leader is one who knows the way, goes the way, and shows the way." This principle emphasizes the essentiality of exceptional leadership.

In today's fast-paced business world, leaders who can navigate complexity, foster engagement, and inspire performance are indispensable. True leaders inspire, innovate, and navigate the ever-evolving workplace landscape by fostering environments where teams can thrive. These leaders are proactive, foster collaboration, encourage innovation, and invest in their team's growth. They create environments that promote communication, psychological safety, and continuous learning.

According to a study by McKinsey & Company, companies with high-performing leadership teams are 2.3 times more likely to outperform their peers in financial performance. One of the leaders who has inspired me greatly is Satya Nadella, CEO of Microsoft. Nadella's transformational leadership approach has been pivotal in reviving Microsoft's culture and performance. When he took over as CEO in 2014, Microsoft faced stagnation. Under his leadership, he was able to shift Microsoft's culture from a competitive, "know-it-all" mindset to a collaborative, "learn-it-all" approach. He steered the company toward cloud computing, artificial intelligence, and other emerging technologies.

Nadella emphasized empathy, inclusion, and empowerment and created a culture that values every employee's contribution. This leadership shift translated into astounding business success: Microsoft's market capitalization grew from around $300 billion in 2014 to over $2 trillion in 2021. It's amazing how such an organization can achieve this with exceptional leadership.

Exceptional leadership begins with strategic hiring practices that align talent acquisition with organizational goals. As a leader, you must be able to carefully define roles and identify skill sets essential for both immediate and future needs. Beyond qualifications, cultural fit becomes a key hiring criterion. Go for individuals who embody organizational values and exhibit a willingness to learn and grow.

Data from LinkedIn's Global Talent Trends report shows that 89% of hiring failures are due to poor cultural fit rather than lack of technical ability. As a leader, you must be able to see beyond the hard skill set of talent and determine the flexibility to fit into the culture of the organization. This is because having the right people who believe in your organizational goal and are ready to work with you is better than skilled talents who are rigid and lack soft skills. However, this is not an attempt to downgrade the importance of hard skills.

Furthermore, it only takes an exceptional leader to attract and retain top talent. It is essential you understand that attracting and retaining top talent requires more than competitive salaries, it demands a work environment where individuals feel valued and empowered. It deals with creating an inclusive environment where diverse perspectives thrive, driving innovation and engagement.

Diversity and inclusion are not just words; they are powerful enablers of innovation and creativity and are highly vital, especially if you manage a large number of employees in order to make them feel comfortable to work and contribute to organizational success.

Also, Gallup's research reveals that employees who strongly agree their manager supports their development are 3.6 times more likely to be engaged than those who don't. You must understand that great talent and a culture that fosters creativity and productivity are indispensable skills to seek in candidates. When you invest in employee development and engagement, you will definitely reap significant rewards, which include higher productivity, innovation, and loyalty.

My Journey in Executive Search

My path to becoming a trusted partner in executive search and leadership strategy was neither linear nor without its lessons. As the founder and driving force behind Innovex, a global company known for its transparent processes and global expertise in helping supporting businesses find the leadership team to accelerate growth.

I've had the privilege of working with global corporations, high-growth startups, and family-owned businesses to identify and place transformative leaders. With over a decade of experience, I've witnessed firsthand how the right leader can revolutionize a business and unlock its untapped potential.

But success didn't come overnight. Early in my career, I struggled with delivering difficult feedback, a challenge many professionals can relate to. In one memorable instance, a client was determined to hire a candidate I believed was a poor cultural fit. The decision weighed heavily on me, but I ultimately chose to voice my honest concerns, even though it required me not to charge the placement fee at that moment, for we had to go back and find another suitable person. My honest communication converted this client into one of our biggest long-term clients in the business.

That experience taught me a critical lesson, which was transparency and candid communication are foundational to building trust and delivering lasting value. Leaders must not only have the courage to make tough decisions but also the integrity to communicate those decisions clearly and openly.

The Purpose of This Book

This book is designed to be a practical resource for:

- Identifying Exceptional Leaders: Understanding what makes a leader not just effective but transformational.
- Building High-Performing Teams: Creating a culture where innovation and collaboration drive success.
- Retaining Top Talent: Develop strategies to keep your leadership team engaged and aligned with your organization's vision.

Through real-world anecdotes, actionable strategies, and a candid exploration of the complexities of leadership, my goal is to provide you with the tools to:

- Make Confident Decisions: Whether selecting a new executive or navigating organizational challenges, understanding the nuances of leadership decision-making is important.
- Foster Growth: By aligning leadership strategies with your business objectives, you can create a foundation for sustained success.
- Unlock Organizational Potential: The right leaders can inspire teams, drive innovation, and navigate complex

challenges with clarity and purpose.

Whether you're an executive seeking to build a winning leadership team, an HR professional tasked with retention strategies, or a business leader navigating organizational transformation, this book is your guide to mastering the art and science of leadership.

Join me on this journey as we explore the key principles for identifying, nurturing, and retaining the leaders who will shape the future of your organization. Together, we'll unlock the strategies that empower you to build an organization where talent thrives and success is sustainable.

1

Who This Book Is For: Understanding the Challenges Faced by Founders, Leaders, and Boards

Most people feel leadership is just about being in control, wielding authority and bossing everyone around to ensure they are doing the right thing. Exceptional leadership goes beyond all these, and it embodies the responsibility of nurturing teams, aligning goals, and steering organizations toward success.

This principle resonates deeply with my work at Innovex and forms the cornerstone of this book. In industries where leadership is the differentiating factor between thriving or merely surviving, identifying and cultivating the right leaders is highly important.

Who This Book Is For

- **Founders and Entrepreneurs:** This book provides strategies for scaling businesses while maintaining operational efficiency. It offers insights on attracting top leadership talent, fostering innovation, and using real-world case studies to turn vision into reality.
- **Corporate Leaders:** Leaders in established organizations will learn how to align leadership efforts with business goals, adapt to market competition, and build high-performing teams that drive sustainable growth and innovation.
- **Private Equity and Venture Capital Firms:** Investors will discover how strong leadership impacts investment success. The book offers techniques for assessing executive teams, optimizing leadership structures, and fostering a culture of operational excellence.
- **Family-Owned Businesses:** Effective leadership transitions are key to long-term success. This book guides family businesses on balancing tradition with innovation, developing future leaders, and sustaining their legacy across generations.
- **Non-Profit and Mission-Driven Entities:** Leadership alignment is crucial for maximizing impact in resource-constrained environments. This book provides tools for enhancing governance, optimizing resources, and driving mission success.

Target Market

Industries, where exceptional leadership drives innovation, growth, and competitive advantage, are the primary focus of this book. From financial services to cybersecurity, SaaS, fintech, insurtech, satellite telecommunication, defense, healthcare and consumer goods, these sectors require leaders who can navigate complexity, drive innovation, and adapt swiftly to evolving market demands. As rapid technological advancements, regulatory challenges, and changing customer expectations shape the business landscape, the ability to lead effectively has never been more critical.

Leaders and decision-makers in financial services will discover strategies to manage governance and compliance challenges while fostering innovation in a highly regulated industry. With digital disruption transforming traditional business models, you must learn to adopt forward-thinking strategies to stay competitive. You will need to develop agile leadership teams and align corporate strategy with board engagement to navigate these challenges.

The technology sector, characterized by constant evolution and fierce competition, demands leaders who can balance rapid innovation with operational stability. Whether driving breakthroughs in artificial intelligence, scaling SaaS platforms, or managing cybersecurity threats, you have to be excellent at building innovative and resilient teams that can manage growth while maintaining the agility and creativity to stay ahead of your competitors.

In the cybersecurity sector, leaders face a relentless landscape of evolving threats and sophisticated attacks. The ability to anticipate, detect, and mitigate security risks is paramount. This book provides insights into building robust security frameworks, promoting a culture of security awareness, and integrating cybersecurity considerations into strategic decision-making.

Also, fintech and insurtech leaders are at the forefront of financial transformation, which is redefining customer experiences and operational efficiencies. With traditional banking models under pressure, leaders must embrace data analytics, blockchain technologies, and machine learning to gain a competitive edge. The book highlights strategies for navigating regulatory landscapes and creating customer-centric solutions that drive market leadership.

In the same light, leaders in satellite telecommunications and defense sectors operate in environments marked by technological advancements and geopolitical complexities. Strategic foresight, mission alignment, and innovation are essential for maintaining operational excellence. To strive in this sector, you must understand the power of collaboration and know how to create a culture that supports technological advancements and ensures robust risk management strategies in organizations.

Conversely, healthcare leaders operate in a field where patient outcomes and regulatory compliance converge with financial performance and technological innovation. As the industry undergoes significant transformation, from telemedicine to data-driven diagnostics, leaders are faced with pressure to innovate while maintaining the highest standards of care. To be able to do that you will have to learn how to create collaborative environments and align leadership with mission-driven goals.

In consumer goods, where market trends shift rapidly and customer demands evolve, leaders must continually innovate while ensuring supply chain efficiency and brand loyalty. By exploring case studies of organizations that have successfully navigated market changes, this book provides practical approaches to building leadership teams that can anticipate trends, maintain operational excellence, and deliver exceptional customer experiences.

Beyond these industries, this book is also a valuable resource for leaders in family-owned enterprises, mission-driven non-profits, and private equity firms. Whether managing leadership transitions, encouraging innovation, or aligning teams to strategic goals, leaders across sectors will find solutions tailored to their specific challenges.

The Challenges Faced by Founders, Leaders, and Boards

Due to the fast-paced and complex nature of the business environment, founders, leaders, and boards face numerous challenges that require strategic vision, adaptability, and strong leadership. It is important to identify and understand these challenges, as it is only then can you will be able to provide the right solution to them. Some of the common challenges faced by founders, leaders, and boards include the following:

1. Talent Acquisition and Retention: The Battle for Leadership Excellence:

Finding and retaining top leadership talent is one of the most pressing challenges for businesses. The business environment is wide and competitive, and professionals are looking out for the organizations that best fit their ideology and can support their professional growth.

With an increasingly competitive talent market, leaders must adopt creative approaches to attract the right people. The demand for high-caliber leaders is fierce, and you must offer compelling value propositions to win over these leaders. This includes not only attractive compensation packages but also opportunities for growth, meaningful work, and alignment with corporate values. Your work environment should be inclusive and supportive of professional advancement.

For instance, Google is renowned for its emphasis on innovation, collaboration, and continuous learning. Salesforce is known for its "Ohana" culture, which promotes family-like support; Microsoft, the "learn-it-all" culture; HubSpot, the "customer-first, employee-second" workplace culture; and Patagonia, its environmental activism, employee well-being, and work-life balance culture. So, you must cultivate that unique culture of your company so that when they think of your company, the idea of the environmental culture comes to their minds.

Retaining talent is equally critical. Gallup's research shows that businesses with highly engaged teams achieve 21% greater profitability. Companies that prioritize leadership development and foster a culture of continuous learning often fare better in the retention game. Investing in leadership pipelines, mentorship programs, and robust succession planning helps mitigate the risks of leadership attrition.

2. Cultural Alignment: Harmonizing Leadership and Organizational Values

Cultural fit and alignment play a pivotal role in leadership effectiveness. Even the most qualified leaders still struggle if they cannot integrate seamlessly into the organization's culture. Founders and leaders must ensure that they employ professionals who not only possess the technical expertise required for the role but also embody the organization's values and cultural ethos. You, as a leader, must culturally align with organizational values; whether you're the founder or corporate executive, it does matter.

A study by LinkedIn found that 89% of hiring failures are due to cultural misfits rather than a lack of technical ability. Leaders who are culturally aligned with their organizations are better positioned to inspire their teams, drive engagement, and encourage innovation. When leaders and employees are unable to align with the culture of the workplace, morale suffers, and this can lead to increased employee turnover and decreased productivity.

To address this challenge, companies must clearly define and communicate their values during the hiring process and seek professionals who resonate with those principles. Creating an inclusive culture where diverse perspectives are valued and respected is essential.

Microsoft CEO Satya Nadella's leadership transformation of the company serves as a prime example. By shifting Microsoft's culture to embrace a "learn-it-all" mindset rather than a "know-it-all" one, Nadella fostered collaboration, innovation, and inclusivity, which are the key drivers of Microsoft's resurgence as a technology leader.

3. Strategic Leadership Transitions: Maintaining Stability During Change

The major problem most founders, leaders and boards of directors face is leadership transitions, as it can be destabilizing if not managed effectively. Whether it's a planned succession or an unexpected departure, ensuring continuity and maintaining momentum is critical to ensure the stability of the organization. If these transitions are poorly managed, they can disrupt operations, affect employee morale, and damage stakeholder confidence.

This is why many founders become scared of what may happen to the organization when they step down or retire, and someone will need to succeed them. However, you have to understand that this becomes a problem only when there is no careful planning and communication.

Successful transitions require careful planning and communication. Boards must proactively identify potential successors and establish transition plans well before leadership changes are needed. As a leader, in whatever capacity you are, you are to be actively training at least three people who can fit into your position when you retire, get transferred or step down. This helps to ensure there is no vacuum left when you leave. Research by Spencer Stuart shows that companies with a formal succession planning process achieve a 20% higher market performance than those without one.

4. Governance and Compliance: Navigating Complex Regulatory Landscapes

Boards of directors play critical roles in ensuring organizations operate transparently and adhere to regulatory requirements. As the regulatory environments grow increasingly complex, especially those in the finance, health, agriculture and tech sectors, effective governance is paramount. Failure to comply with regulations can result in reputational damage, financial penalties, and operational disruptions.

A PwC study revealed that 72% of directors believe that regulatory complexity has increased substantially over the past three years. Understanding and keeping track of the evolving regulations has been daunting, and most leaders have mistakenly attracted penalties on the organization due to a lack of proper understanding and being current with the regulations.

To address these governance challenges, the board must ensure that they have the right mix of skills, expertise, and independence to effectively oversee management and safeguard shareholder interests. Moreover, creating an environment of transparency and accountability is essential for maintaining trust with stakeholders.

Also, organizations must adopt robust frameworks for compliance monitoring, risk management, and reporting. Effective board evaluations and ongoing education for directors help educate them and ensure they are always equipped to navigate the evolving regulatory landscape.

5. Innovation and Adaptation: Balancing Innovation and Operational Excellence

In an age of rapid technological advancement, the ability to innovate and adapt is critical to staying ahead of market trends. However, most founders and leaders are faced with the problem of maintaining a balance between operational stability and creating an environment conducive to experimentation and innovation. There must be a balance between these two, or else the organization will suffer in some ways.

Successful companies have been able to balance innovation with operational excellence such as SpaceX and Toyota and this has kept them as leaders in their industry. Do not just say these organizations are big, so they cannot be replicated in your startup or mid-size industry. These organizations start small and grow due to their focus on innovation and operational excellence, and you can also do so. As you continue in this book, you will learn practical strategies that will significantly help you incorporate processes in your workplace to ensure balance.

Key Takeaway

- True leadership is about nurturing teams, aligning goals, and driving organizational success, not just exercising control.

WHO THIS BOOK IS FOR: UNDERSTANDING THE CHALLENGES FACED BY...

- Designed for founders, leaders, investors, family business owners, and non-profit leaders seeking strategic leadership insights, Innovex is renowned for developing high-performing leadership teams.
- Innovex guides scaling, assembling high-performing teams, and sustaining long-term business success across private equity and family-owned businesses,
- Innovex equips mission-driven entities with strategies for governance, alignment, and maximizing impact.
- Backed by Innovex's leadership consulting, helping organizations build resilient and visionary leaders.
- Innovex's four-week shortlist guarantee, transparent processes, and global expertise help organizations build resilient and visionary leaders.

2

About the Author: My Experience, Expertise, and Lessons in Transforming Organizations

As a leadership consultant, my professional journey has been one of transformation, not just for the organizations I've worked with but also for myself. Over the years, I have come to understand that leadership is not about being at the top of an organizational pyramid but about cultivating environments that enable others to thrive and lead in their own right. This philosophy has guided my work and shaped my approach to overcoming the complex challenges that organizations face.

Through a combination of personal anecdotes and case studies, I will reflect on the lessons I have learned throughout my career in transforming businesses, enhancing leadership capabilities, and driving lasting change.

My Journey in Leadership Consulting

One of the most formative experiences in my career as a consultant occurred early on when I faced a situation that tested both my professional integrity and my communication skills. A client, an established company in need of leadership support, had identified a potential candidate to hire for a key position within their organization. I reinforced some of the constructive feedback to consider that it was a lack of cultural fit. Despite not charging the final fee, I had the client's best interests at heart, so the client ended up listening, and we found a more suitable candidate who then made a significant impact and didn't just fit into the culture but improved it. I learned early on that this approach was the one to take to build long-lasting relationships.

That moment was pivotal in my growth as a consultant. I learned a major lesson that very day and it was the power of candid and transparent communication. By being honest and forthright, I not only prevented a costly hiring mistake but also gained the trust and respect of my client. This experience taught me that I need to courageously speak the truth even though the situation is challenging and it is not comfortable. This realization has been foundational to my approach to consulting, and from that day onwards, I always prioritize open and honest communication with clients.

Overcoming the Challenge of Scaling Innovex

Another personal anecdote that shaped my consulting philosophy occurred when I founded Innovex, a business consulting firm specializing in leadership and organizational development.

The experience of scaling Innovex was both rewarding and challenging. Like many entrepreneurs, I encountered obstacles that tested my resilience and problem-solving abilities. One of the most significant challenges came when we over committed resources to a large-scale project, which led to significant delays that compromised the quality of our work.

This setback reminded me of the complexities involved in scaling a business. It forced me to confront my assumptions about growth, particularly the idea that increased volume automatically translates to success. After careful analysis, I identified key areas where our processes were inefficient. In particular, our resource management and project timelines needed to be re-calibrated. I realized that scaling wasn't just about increasing output. It required the ability to maintain quality while expanding operations. After identifying the problem, I know I need to address it.

To address these issues, I implemented several strategic changes. First, we streamlined our processes and focused on improving workflow efficiency. I introduced project management software that allowed us to better allocate resources and track timelines. Furthermore, we invested in technology to automate routine tasks, and this freed up my employees to be able to focus on strategic initiatives. These improvements led to a remarkable turnaround. Not only did we meet our project deadlines, but we also doubled our operational efficiency, which significantly enhanced client satisfaction.

A major lesson I learned from this experience is that scaling a business is not just about growth in numbers but about ensuring that the infrastructure, processes, and culture can support that growth. As a result, I adopted a more strategic approach to growth, one that prioritized sustainability and operational efficiency. These lessons have not only helped build up my organization but have also informed my consulting practice, where I now emphasize the importance of scalable systems and processes to my clients, which has greatly helped them navigate the complexities of growth while maintaining the integrity of their business operations.

Lessons Learned in Transforming Organizations

Case Study: Transforming a Stagnant Board into a High-Performing Team

One of the most rewarding projects I've worked on involved helping a global financial services firm address the dysfunctionality of its board. The company's board was struggling with alignment and strategic decision-making, and this often led to lengthy debates that birth no results or definite consensus.

The board's lack of direction was hindering the organization's ability to make crucial strategic decisions, and this was gradually affecting the firm's performance. In this case, the challenge was clear and the problem was glaring, and it was that the board lacked cohesion and a shared understanding of its role within the organization. Working closely with the CEO, I began by conducting an in-depth assessment of the board's skills, governance structures, and communication practices. Through this process, we identified several critical gaps, which included a lack of diversity in skill sets and an absence of effective communication strategies.

To address these issues, we started with reshaping the board's composition. I guided the CEO through a targeted recruitment process that sought out individuals who possessed the necessary skills and experience to complement the existing team. We also implemented regular strategy workshops that were designed not only to align the board with the company's vision but also to teach the employees good communication and decision-making skills and processes. These workshops facilitated open dialogue among board members, which enabled them to express their perspectives and reach decisions more efficiently.

Within a year of implementing these changes, the firm saw a 15% increase in organizational performance. The board became more cohesive, strategic, and proactive, and the firm was able to make critical decisions that helped drive business growth.

This case further exemplifies and helped me understand the importance of proactive board management and the impact that well-structured governance can have on an organization's performance. In my experience, many organizations fail to recognize the significance of board dynamics until performance begins to slip. In as much as it is necessary to have the right talents, you have to ensure that you have the right people on your board of leaders or directors. This case taught me that effective governance is not a luxury but a necessity for high-performing organizations.

Case Study: Retaining Talent During a Leadership Transition

Another case that stands out in my career involved helping a high-growth tech company navigate a leadership transition. The company was undergoing a change in leadership from its founder to a new CEO, and the transition became challenging.

One of the primary concerns was the potential exit of key leaders who had been with the company since its inception. Many of the leaders that were inducted were new and unsure of their future with the company, as such, they refused to commit to the organization as expected.

Recognizing the importance of retaining this talent, I worked with the company's leadership team to design a comprehensive retention strategy. The strategy focused on three key areas: transparent communication, personalized development plans, and equity incentives. We held several sections of town hall meetings where the new CEO could share his vision for the company, address concerns, and offer clarity about the company's direction.

In addition, I worked with the new CEO in drafting personalized development plans for each executive, clearly stating the opportunities for growth and advancement that each leadership comes with. Also, we introduced equity incentives to ensure that key leaders were financially motivated to stay with the company long-term.

Upon receiving these development plans and the offer of quality incentives, the new leaders have a change of mindset and become very optimistic about the company, and this positively influences their commitment and dedication.

Simply, the results were impressive. 90% of the old leadership team stayed with the company through the transition, and the company was able to maintain stability during a period of uncertainty. This experience highlighted the importance of having a well-thought-out retention strategy. It also reinforced the value of clear communication and trust-building, which can help ease transitions and maintain organizational continuity.

Reflection and Moving Forward

Through these cases and personal experiences, I have gained invaluable insights into the challenges and opportunities faced by leaders and organizations. My journey as a leadership consultant has taught me that no two organizations are alike, and each requires a tailored approach to leadership development and organizational change. Whether transforming a stagnant board, helping a company retain talent, or scaling a business, my work is rooted in the belief that successful transformation requires more than just strategy—it requires the alignment of people, processes, and culture.

As I continue to work with clients, I remain committed to providing actionable insights that help organizations navigate change and achieve sustainable growth. My expertise lies in understanding the nuances of organizational dynamics and developing customized strategies that address the unique needs of each client. By focusing on effective communication, strategic alignment, and process improvement, I aim to create environments where organizations can thrive and achieve long-term success.

A key advantage I bring to every partnership is Innovex's strengths, such as the four-week shortlist guarantee, transparent processes, and global expertise. These elements ensure that the solutions we provide are not only efficient and timely but also crafted with a deep understanding of global leadership trends and challenges. With Innovex, clients can trust in a structured, transparent approach that accelerates results and supports long-term growth.

Looking ahead, I am excited to continue applying these strengths, tailoring solutions to each organization's specific needs, and creating environments where they can thrive sustainably.

Key Takeaway

- Leadership is not about being at the top but about creating environments where others can lead and thrive.
- Create a culture where leadership is nurtured at all levels. Focus on building systems that support the growth of employees as leaders.
- Practice open, honest communication in every business relationship to foster trust and ensure long-term success.
- Assess your infrastructure and operations thoroughly before scaling. Identify gaps and invest in technology and processes that support sustainable growth.
- Focus on recruiting the right talent for your board. Imple-

ment regular strategy sessions and ensure diverse skills for more effective decision-making.

- Tailor your leadership strategies to fit the unique needs of your organization. Take the time to assess organizational dynamics before implementing change.
- Ensure that all three elements are aligned when driving transformation. This holistic approach is key to long-term success.
- Utilize Innovex's global expertise, transparent processes, and the four-week shortlist guarantee to ensure timely and effective organizational solutions. This approach accelerates results and supports sustainable growth.

3

The Value You'll Gain from this book

This book is enriched with tools, strategies, and insights to tackle your leadership challenges head-on and drive success. Three major areas will be covered in this book that will empower you to be that visionary leader. You have always aimed to include clarity in leadership decisions, enhanced organizational effectiveness and sustainable growth strategies. We will look at what these entail in this section and the subsequent chapters.

Clarity in Leadership Decisions

Fundamentally, effective leadership is about making decisions that not only benefit the organization in the present but also set the stage for future success. In making decisions, you have to ensure that they align with the balance of innovation and operational efficiency of the present and the possibility of scaling. To be able to do that, you must have clarity. As such, clarity in leadership decisions serves as the cornerstone of this process. It is the ability to make choices with confidence, understanding their implications on both short-term goals and long-term vision.

A lack of clarity in decision-making can lead to imbalance, confusion, disengagement, and missed opportunities, which can affect the organization's success. In contrast, leaders who make clear and informed decisions cultivate a sense of direction and purpose within their teams, and this creates an environment where every team member knows their role and the level of commitment that is expected of each of them.

One of the most challenging aspects of leadership is making decisions in high-pressure and high-stakes situations. The ability to assess multiple variables, weigh risks, and choose the best path forward is highly essential. Clarity in decision-making isn't just about making the "right" decision; it's also about ensuring that the decision aligns with the organization's broader objectives, vision, and values. As a leader, you build trust and inspire confidence in your teams when your decisions are aligned with these guiding principles. This gives them the confidence that you, as a leader, are focused and know what to do; as such, they are able to trust you. You get your teams to lose confidence in you when they observe that your decisions are always inconsistent with the organizational goals.

Effective decision-making is not a skill that you develop overnight. It requires having a strong foundation of self-awareness, emotional intelligence, and an understanding of the organization's long-term vision.

To exhibit clarity in your decisions, you must recognize that good decisions require both strategic foresight and the ability to learn from past experiences. This self-reflective approach allows you to improve your decision-making process continuously and take into cognizance new information and evolving circumstances.

Identifying and Attracting Top Talent

One of the most critical decisions leaders face is identifying and attracting the right talent. The people you hire directly influence your organization's ability to meet its goals and succeed in a competitive marketplace. In fact, McKinsey & Company's research has shown that organizations with strong talent acquisition processes are 2.5 times more likely to outperform their competitors in profitability and productivity. This finding shows the huge importance of a well-thought-out recruitment strategy, one that goes beyond simply filling positions but instead focuses on finding individuals who are aligned with the organization's mission and values. In the previous chapter, I emphasized that in as much as hard skill is essential, determining the ability of the candidate to fit into the organization's culture is equally important.

To identify top talent, you need to have a deep understanding of the skills, experiences, and qualities that are necessary for the organization to succeed. It's not just about hiring people who have the technical expertise for the job but about looking for candidates who possess the ability to contribute to the culture and vision of the organization. In my work as a leadership consultant, I have encountered many organizations that prioritize speed over strategy when it comes to hiring. While quick hires might fill immediate gaps, they often do not fit the long-term needs of the organization and this often leads to turnover, disengagement, and loss of valuable talent.

For example, early in my consulting career, I worked with a rapidly expanding tech startup that was struggling to scale. Their hiring process was swift, but it lacked a clear strategy. As a result, the company was hiring individuals based on immediate needs rather than long-term potential, and many of these new hires did not integrate well into the company culture. This mismatch led to high turnover and decreased morale, and this affected the company's ability to grow.

I introduced the company to a competency-based hiring process, which focused on employing candidates who not only had the technical skills required but also the cultural fit necessary for the organization to thrive. This shift in strategy led to a dramatic improvement in both employee retention and the performance of the workforce.

Aligning Talent with Your Vision

Attracting top-tier talent is only the first step in building a high-performing team. Once the right individuals are in place, you have to ensure that they properly understand the organization's mission, vision, and values. This alignment is vital for promoting long-term engagement and ensuring that employees are not just working for a paycheck but are committed to the organization's success.

Employees are more likely to be fully engaged and motivated when they observe that there is a connection between their values and the organization's mission. This is why it is critical for leaders to communicate the company's vision clearly and to involve employees in the organization's goals. Engaged employees are more productive, more innovative, and more likely to stay with the company.

Throughout my career, I have emphasized the importance of alignment between individual talent and organizational purpose. I've worked with numerous clients who, although they had hired skilled individuals, struggled to retain them because these employees didn't feel personally connected to the company's goals.

A prime example of this occurred with a mid-sized manufacturing company that struggled to engage its workforce despite offering competitive salaries and benefits. When I worked with the leadership team, we identified a lack of alignment between employees' work and the company's mission, which created a sense of disconnect. We worked on redefining the company's values and vision and made sure that employees understood how their roles contributed to achieving these larger goals. This clarity influenced the mindset of the employees and, as such, impacted their morale, which led to increased productivity.

Leaders can facilitate this alignment and create a culture where employees are regularly reminded of what is expected of them in the organization. One way to do this is by creating regular opportunities for open dialogue, feedback, and collaborative decision-making. Give your employees the allowance to openly discuss their concerns and ideas. Doing this helped them know that you value and respect them, and they tend to be more emotionally involved in the organization.

Furthermore, encourage your employees to see the bigger picture by connecting their day-to-day responsibilities to the company's overarching mission. For example, instead of merely asking them to meet production targets, explain how their work supports the company's larger purpose of creating value for customers or improving the community.

To further strengthen this alignment, I advise leaders to provide ongoing professional development opportunities that help employees grow in line with both their personal goals and the organization's objectives. The beauty of such investment in development is that they not only enhance individual performance but also strengthen the organization as a whole.

The Role of Clear Leadership in Talent Retention

While attracting top talent is a critical aspect of leadership, retaining that talent is equally important. Employees who feel supported, valued, and aligned with their organization's mission are far less likely to leave. In contrast, a lack of clarity in leadership decisions can lead to confusion, frustration, and disengagement, all of which contribute to turnover.

Clear leadership decisions help you to establish expectations, build trust, and provide direction, all of which are needed to retain high-performing employees. As a leader, you need to be cautious when stating the benefits candidates are to enjoy while working with you so that you don't end up over-promising and under-delivering. This can make high-potential employees

THE VALUE YOU'LL GAIN FROM THIS BOOK

feel cheated and lied to, and they will want to leave. Ensure you are clear about fulfilling the stated benefits you outline to your employees. (I will discuss further key Leadership Challenges in Identifying the Right Talent in a Competitive Market and proven retention strategies in section 6).

Enhanced Board Effectiveness

Another major benefit you will have from reading this book is learning to enhance your board effectiveness, for it is an essential ingredient for organizational success. Boards provide critical oversight, strategy, and governance to keep the organization on course and achieve its long-term goals.

However, to truly capitalize on the strengths of a board, it is necessary to develop strategies that enhance its effectiveness. This requires not only selecting the right individuals but also creating an environment that encourages collaboration, transparency, and a shared vision.

A study by Harvard Business Review highlights that effective boards play an essential role in driving corporate success by providing the guidance necessary for leaders to make informed decisions. This study emphasizes that high-performing boards contribute to better strategic decision-making, more effective risk management, and stronger financial outcomes. A board that is composed of individuals with diverse skills, expertise, and perspectives can bring valuable insights to the table, which strengthens the organization to navigate complex challenges and seize growth opportunities.

The board's role goes beyond just financial oversight. It is also responsible for keeping the organization's strategy aligned with its vision and mission while also holding leaders accountable for the execution of that strategy. When a board is functioning at its highest level, its collective decision-making power can help steer an organization to new heights of success.

Several established models provide leaders with the tools and structure needed to address organizational challenges and ensure enhanced board effectiveness. In my experience as a leadership consultant, applying these models can significantly improve decision-making processes and optimize organizational performance. In section 7, we will explore the three critical models that I frequently use, which are the McKinsey 7-S Framework, Tuckman's Stages of Team Development, and Kotter's 8-Step Change Model.

Actionable Insights and Case Studies

Throughout my career, I've had the opportunity to work with a wide range of businesses, each facing unique obstacles. By sharing their stories, I want the readers to gain insights from these concrete examples of how the strategies discussed can lead to tangible results and provide them with the confidence to navigate similar challenges in their leadership journeys. In Chapter 8, we will dig into various case studies and what lessons can be drawn from them.

Checklist:

The Value of Time

- Time is a scarce and invaluable resource for any leader.
- With increasing leadership demands, it's crucial to make swift, informed decisions while maintaining high performance.

Streamlining Decision-Making

- By applying the strategies and techniques discussed in this book, leaders can streamline their decision-making processes.
- These methods reduce inefficiencies, eliminate guesswork, and allow leaders to focus on what truly matters: achieving their organization's goals.

Managing Competing Priorities

- Leaders often face pressure to juggle multiple priorities, such as managing teams, overseeing operations, meeting deadlines, and handling unexpected challenges.
- Proper time management helps reduce stress and improve organizational outcomes.

Implementing Structured Frameworks

- A highly effective time-saving strategy is using structured frameworks.
- These frameworks provide a systematic approach to problem-solving and decision-making, making tasks more manageable.

- In upcoming chapters, we will explore how frameworks like the McKinsey 7-S Model and Tuckman's Stages of Team Development can save time.

Effective Communication Techniques

- Miscommunication is a major productivity killer. When leaders fail to communicate clearly, they waste time revisiting issues and clarifying misunderstandings.
- To address this, we will discuss communication tools such as the SBAR technique (Situation, Background, Assessment, Recommendation) and the Daily Stand-up Meetings strategy.

Decision-Making Models

- We will also explore decision-making models that can save time, such as:
- Eisenhower Matrix: A method for prioritizing tasks based on urgency and importance.
- OODA Loop (Observe, Orient, Decide, Act): A model for rapid decision-making in dynamic situations.

Delegation Matrices

- Effective delegation is another time-saving strategy. The RACI Model (Responsible, Accountable, Consulted, Informed) helps leaders assign and manage tasks.

Automation Tools

- Technology enables leaders to automate repetitive tasks, saving valuable time.
- Automation tools like Zapier or Microsoft Power Automate can handle tasks such as transferring data, scheduling meetings, or generating reports.
- AI-driven tools can further help with workflows, sending reminders, or following up on tasks.

Personal and Professional Growth

One of the greatest benefits of reading this book is the opportunity for both personal and professional growth. Leadership is not merely about managing people or making strategic decisions. It is a journey of continuous improvement, learning, and adaptation. In leadership, you don't just lead; you become a better person yourself.

Furthermore, effective leadership requires a growth mindset, one that prioritizes self-awareness, resilience, and the ability to evolve in response to both challenges and opportunities. This book is designed to help you develop those qualities, which empowers you to become the type of leader who not only drives organizational success but also sponsors growth within yourself and those around you.

Continuous Learning and Adaptation

Leadership is not static. The business world is constantly evolving, and so too must the leaders who navigate it. This has made continuous learning invaluable for staying relevant and effective. This book emphasizes the importance of ongoing professional development, whether through formal education, mentorship, or self-directed learning. By incorporating strategies such as leadership training, reading, and networking into your routine, you can cultivate the skills necessary to adapt to new challenges and stay ahead of industry trends.

The Leadership Pipeline Chart that will be discussed in this book is an excellent tool for understanding how leadership development should evolve. This chart not only helps you track your progression as a leader but also enables you to identify areas where you need further development. Whether it's improving your communication skills, mastering strategic decision-making, or learning how to navigate complex team dynamics, this framework helps ensure that you are always learning and improving.

Gaining Confidence in Your Leadership Abilities

One of the most empowering aspects of leadership is the ability to make informed decisions with confidence. Leaders who are continuously growing both personally and professionally are more likely to make decisions that align with the organization's goals and values. When you embrace the tools, techniques, and frameworks outlined in this book, you will gain a stronger sense of self-assurance in your leadership abilities. Furthermore, you will learn to inspire and empower yourself.

As a leader, your growth is not only about personal achievement—it's also about empowering those around you. In addition to all the benefits you will attain from this book, you will learn to be a true learner, one who grows and invests in people, helping them achieve their potential.

As you grow in your leadership journey, you will be empowered to create meaningful change that endures and build a legacy of success and empowerment for your organization and beyond.

Key Takeaways

Clarity in Leadership Decisions

- Clear decision-making is crucial for organizational success, ensuring alignment with both present operational needs and future growth.
- Leaders must make informed decisions that balance innovation and operational efficiency, considering the long-term vision of the organization.
- A lack of clarity in decision-making leads to confusion, disengagement, and missed opportunities, while clarity builds trust and confidence within teams.
- Innovex Global offers cutting-edge tools and systems that enhance and equip leaders to have better decision-making processes.

Identifying and Attracting Top Talent

- A strong recruitment strategy goes beyond filling positions; it focuses on hiring individuals who align with the organization's culture and long-term goals.
- Hiring speed without a clear strategy can lead to mismatches in culture and long-term fit, affecting retention and performance.
- Innovex provides recruitment and talent management platforms that streamline the hiring process and help companies attract top-tier talent that aligns with organizational culture and values.

Aligning Talent with Your Vision

- Once the right talent is hired, ensuring alignment with the organization's mission, vision, and values is essential for long-term employee engagement.
- Employees are more motivated when they see a connection between their values and the organization's goals.
- Clear communication of the company's vision and the involvement of employees in goal-setting fosters engagement and higher productivity.
- Innovex offers employee engagement tools that align individual talent with organizational goals and help leaders have a better understanding of employee aspirations, skill sets, and motivations.

The Role of Clear Leadership in Talent Retention

- Retaining top talent requires clear leadership, which helps establish expectations, build trust, and provide direction.
- Over-promising benefits and not fulfilling them can lead to dissatisfaction and high turnover; clear, honest communication is essential for retention.
- Innovex provides robust HR tools that ensure transparency, clarity, and consistency in leadership communication, which helps you to track employee progress, set clear expectations, and provide timely feedback.

Enhanced Board Effectiveness

- Effective boards contribute to strategic decision-making, risk management, and overall corporate success by providing valuable insights and guidance.
- A high-functioning board ensures that the organization's strategy remains aligned with its vision and holds leadership accountable.
- Innovex's board management solutions provide tools for improving governance, transparency, and communication at the board level.

Personal and Professional Growth

- Leadership is a journey of continuous learning and improvement, requiring a growth mindset focused on self-awareness, resilience, and adaptability.
- Ongoing professional development, mentorship, and self-directed learning are essential for staying relevant in a

dynamic business environment.

- Innovex supports continuous leadership development by offering tailored training programs and growth assessments. Its learning management system allows leaders to access resources that cultivate resilience, emotional intelligence, and strategic thinking.

Continuous Learning and Adaptation

- Leadership requires constant adaptation to new challenges, and leaders must invest in continuous learning through training, networking, and self-education.
- Tools like the Leadership Pipeline Chart help track leadership development, identify growth areas, and support ongoing personal and professional growth.
- Innovex encourages lifelong learning through its integrated platform that offers continuous educational resources, mentoring opportunities, and peer networks.

4

The Innovex Approach: From Discovery to Placement, Retention, and Long-Term Success

At Innovex, we adopt a strategic, results-driven process to ensure each client achieves their leadership and organizational goals. Guided by a proven framework, we have been able to deliver exceptional outcomes continuously by seamlessly integrating transparency, insight, and client collaboration at every stage. Here in this section, I will guide you to understanding the strategic process we adopt from discovering candidates to placement, retention, and long-term success.

Discovery and Consultation

Our journey together begins with a deep and thorough exploration of your organization's unique challenges, goals, and culture. As I noted earlier, no two organizations are the same. So, we need to approach each organization uniquely.

The first step in this process is conducting a comprehensive analysis of your current organizational structure, market position, and cultural dynamics. This involves gathering input from all key stakeholders across different levels. It could be through interviews, surveys, and interactive sessions to gain insights into your leadership capabilities, operational pain points, and opportunities for innovation.

Beyond surface-level observations, we dig deeper to uncover the specific problem or root causes that may be hindering progress. It could be a lack of effective communication channels, gaps in leadership development, challenges in aligning teams with strategic goals, or anything else. The identification of the specific problem will enable us to understand the problem at hand and the specific procedures to employ.

In addition to identifying the specific challenge, we clarify your organizational goals to ensure it is aligned with your vision for the future. We explore questions such as:

- What are the key objectives you want to achieve in the next 1, 3, or 5 years?
- How does your leadership team currently support these objectives?
- What cultural or structural shifts are necessary to sustain long-term success?

This helps us to inform the leadership strategies to adopt and recommend to ensure they are directly connected to your broader business goals to create a bridge between aspiration and execution. Furthermore, as part of the discovery process, we evaluate your current leadership framework to assess its readiness to drive change. Our meticulous analysis includes assessing competencies such as:

- Decision-making and strategic thinking
- Communication and conflict resolution skills
- Ability to inspire, motivate, and manage diverse teams
- Capacity for innovation and adaptability to change

Identifying both the strengths and areas for improvement within your leadership team helps us to lay the groundwork for targeted development initiatives. A hallmark of our approach is promoting a culture of open and honest dialogue. We encourage stakeholders to share their perspectives and experiences in order to create a transparent environment.

The insights gathered during the discovery phase inform customized strategies designed to address your specific needs. Our recommendations go beyond generic solutions to solutions that are practical and relevant to your organization.

Innovex Talent Strategy Design

Building on the critical insights gained during the discovery phase, we meticulously design a comprehensive talent strategy to meet your organization's unique needs. This bespoke approach ensures that we align every aspect of the strategy with your broader goals and long-term objectives and ensure that only the right people are employed to fill the positions and prove the expertise that the organization lacks.

The foundation of an effective talent strategy begins with clearly defining the specific roles essential for achieving your strategic vision. We do that by taking a holistic view of both current needs and future aspirations. Each role is carefully mapped out with clear responsibilities, expected contributions, and leadership qualities required. This precision in role definition reduces ambiguity, streamlines the search process, and increases the likelihood of finding candidates who fit seamlessly within your organizational culture.

Furthermore, we establish the success metrics in measuring the effectiveness of each role. You have to understand that measuring the effectiveness of leadership requires more than intuition. It demands clearly defined success metrics that align with your organization's objectives. We help you establish performance indicators that assess both the immediate impact and long-term contributions of leadership roles.

These metrics may include:

- Achievement of strategic business goals
- Team engagement and retention rates
- Innovation and process improvements
- Revenue growth and market expansion
- Cultural alignment and team development

By establishing these benchmarks upfront, we create a transparent framework to evaluate both the recruitment process and leadership effectiveness post-hire.

A critical element of our talent strategy design involves crafting detailed candidate profiles that encapsulate the skills, experiences, and attributes necessary for success. These profiles go beyond technical competencies to include:

- Cultural Fit: Ensuring that candidates share and exemplify your organization's values and mission
- Leadership Style: Identifying candidates who can inspire, lead by example, and work effectively with others.
- Growth Potential: Seeking leaders who can evolve alongside your organization and navigate future challenges
- Diversity and Inclusion: Prioritizing candidates who contribute to a diverse and inclusive workforce

We use these profiles as a blueprint for sourcing, evaluating, and selecting candidates to ensure that every individual considered aligns with your organization's vision for leadership excellence.

Innovex Comprehensive Search and Assessment Framework

After outlining the specific roles needed in the organization, their specific roles, responsibilities, expectations, and success metrics, we proceed with a comprehensive search and assessment of potential hires.

Selecting the right talent goes beyond matching resumes to job descriptions. It requires a thoughtful, comprehensive approach that evaluates both technical qualifications and cultural alignment to ensure a seamless fit with your organization. Our comprehensive search and assessment process combines an extensive network of industry connections with cutting-edge tools and methods.

With years of experience in executive search, we have built a robust network of top-tier talent across industries. This network serves as a valuable resource, which allows us to tap into a diverse pool of candidates who are often not actively seeking new roles but possess the skills and leadership qualities your organization needs. According to a LinkedIn report, 70% of the global workforce is comprised of passive talent, making direct outreach essential for attracting high-caliber candidates.

We engage with potential candidates through targeted sourcing strategies to identify individuals who are both qualified and aligned with your organizational mission. Some people do see that you need to have the right intuition to choose the right candidate. Although this is true in certain cases, you have to understand that identifying the right candidate requires more than intuition; it demands a data-driven approach to assessment. We employ state-of-the-art assessment tools to gain objective insights into candidates' skills, cognitive abilities, leadership potential, and interpersonal qualities. These tools help us measure competencies such as decision-making, strategic thinking, adaptability, and communication effectiveness.

Research by the Harvard Business Review underscores the importance of data-driven hiring decisions, noting that companies using structured assessments are 24% more likely to have high performers in leadership roles. Our comprehensive evaluations ensure that candidates meet your organization's technical and strategic needs.

Assessing Cultural Fit

Cultural fit is a critical element of successful leadership placements. A talent who aligns with your organization's values, communication style, and team dynamics is more likely to put n their best. So, our evaluation process also includes behavioral interviews and scenario-based assessments that reveal how candidates approach problem-solving, team management, and conflict resolution within your organizational context. By understanding candidates' leadership philosophies and communication styles, we assess their ability to integrate seamlessly into your existing culture.

While technical expertise is essential, the ability to build relationships, inspire teams, and communicate effectively is equally important. According to a survey by Deloitte, 92% of leaders believe that soft skills are just as critical as technical skills for successful leadership. Our evaluation process assesses both, ensuring that candidates not only meet the job's technical demands but also possess the interpersonal skills necessary to lead and motivate teams.

Delivering Leaders Aligned with Your Objectives

The culmination of our search and assessment process is the identification of talent who are not only skilled but also aligned with your organization's goals and values.

So, the talent must possess the required hard and soft skills, have the right interpersonal skills, be able to culturally fit into the organization, must have a proper understanding of the

Innovex Leadership Placement Process

organizational goal and values aligned to it.

Innovex Leadership Placement Process

After identifying the ideal candidate through our rigorous search and assessment process, the next critical step is ensuring a smooth and successful leadership placement. The transition from candidate selection to integration into your organization is important. Our leadership placement process goes beyond merely filling a vacancy; it is about facilitating a seamless, well-managed transition that aligns the candidate's goals with those of your organization.

The selection of a leader is a decisive moment for any organization. Our process is designed to eliminate ambiguity and ensure that the best candidate is chosen with clarity and confidence. After thorough evaluation and interviews, we present a clear recommendation to your leadership team, outlining how the candidate aligns with the job's requirements, cultural expectations, and long-term organizational goals.

We understand the weight of this decision and provide you with all the necessary insights, which includes the feedback from stakeholders involved in the interview process. This helps you to have all the data and information you need to make an informed choice. This careful approach helps eliminate risks and sets the stage for a positive future with your new leader.

Once the ideal candidate is selected, we take charge of the offer negotiation process. This stage is often critical as it sets the tone for the candidate's initial experience with your organization.

We work with both the candidate and your HR team to ensure that the offer package is competitive and aligns with both parties' expectations.

Our experience and industry knowledge allow us to guide you through the complexities of compensation, benefits, and other contractual elements. We work to balance the candidate's aspirations with your organization's budget and goals, ensuring that the offer is attractive enough to secure the candidate's commitment while reflecting the value they will bring to your organization.

On boarding and Integration

Successful leadership placement does not end with the acceptance of an offer; it extends into the on boarding and integration phase, which sets a tone for how well the candidates will easily integrate into the organization. Our team helps facilitate this process, ensuring that your new leader is set up for success from day one. We collaborate closely with your HR department to create a tailored on boarding experience that ensures alignment between the leader's goals and the organization's needs.

During this phase, we ensure that the new professional is properly introduced to the team, provided with the resources they need to succeed, and given a clear road map for their first 90 days. A well-structured on boarding process leads to higher employee retention, as research by the Brandon Hall Group suggests that organizations with a strong on boarding process improve new hire retention by 82%.

We also support the new talent in their early interactions with key stakeholders, ensuring they have the right tools and strategies to work seamlessly and build relationships and trust in their teams. Also, this helps us to identify any potential challenges early, providing an opportunity to make adjustments if necessary. This ongoing support is essential for reinforcing the new professional commitment and ensuring they are positioned to drive success.

Innovex Retention and Board Effectiveness Support

At the heart of effective leadership placement lies the ongoing support necessary to ensure long-term success and stability. Our commitment to your organization doesn't end once the ideal candidate is placed. To maximize the impact of your new leader and ensure that they thrive in their role, we offer comprehensive, ongoing advisory services designed to provide retention, enhance leadership performance, and optimize board effectiveness. We do this through several tools to create a foundation for sustainable growth and success.

Leadership coaching is one of the most effective tools to ensure that the new professional continues to evolve and reach their full potential. We recognize that the transition into a leadership role can be challenging, and it's essential that the leader not only adjusts to their new environment but also develops the skills necessary to lead effectively. Our executive coaching programs are tailored to each professional, unique needs, focusing on enhancing key leadership competencies such as decision-making, communication, emotional intelligence, and conflict resolution.

Retention Planning for Long-Term Stability

Through ongoing coaching, we ensure that the new professional has the support and guidance needed to overcome challenges and navigate complex organizational dynamics, which are essential ingredients for success in the current business world.

Retention Planning for Long-Term Stability

Leadership retention is critical to maintaining organizational stability, especially during periods of change or growth. Our retention planning services are designed to help your organization build a strategy that ensures high-performing talents remain engaged and committed to your organization's vision.

We work with your HR team to create customized retention plans that include competitive compensation packages, professional development opportunities, career progression pathways, and work-life balance strategies. Research from Gallup indicates that 70% of employees feel their engagement is influenced by their direct manager's ability to support their development. By aligning leadership goals with employee engagement, we not only retain top talent but also create a thriving and motivated workforce.

Furthermore, retention planning goes beyond financial incentives. We help create a culture that prioritizes recognition, growth opportunities, and alignment between individual and organizational goals, which helps to create a culture where your leaders feel valued and motivated to stay and grow within your company.

Board Alignment Strategies for Organizational Effectiveness

The alignment between the executive team and the board often influences the effectiveness of your leadership. A well-aligned board provides strategic direction, oversight, and support that enables leaders to execute their vision successfully. However, misalignment between the board and leadership can create challenges that undermine organizational growth and stability.

Our board alignment strategies are designed to bridge any gaps between your board's expectations and your leadership team's goals. We work with both boards and leaders to establish clear communication channels, shared objectives, and mutual understanding to create trust, transparency, and strategic alignment.

Studies from McKinsey & Company suggest that companies with highly effective boards experience 20% higher performance growth than those with less effective boards. By ensuring that your board and leadership are aligned, we help your organization make more informed decisions that prioritize initiatives that drive success and a culture of accountability and innovation. As you know, these are essentials for every organization to ensure stable and progressive growth in the current dynamic and fast-paced business world.

Insights and Reporting

At the heart of every successful leadership placement and organizational development strategy is transparency and clear communication. We understand that the ability to make informed decisions is crucial to your organization's success, and that's why we prioritize providing data-driven insights and transparent reporting throughout every phase of our process.

From the initial stages of candidate discovery to leadership placement and ongoing support, our approach centers around providing you with actionable intelligence that enables you to make confident, strategic decisions. Transparency ensures you are always informed about progress, challenges, and opportunities, which allows you to take proactive steps toward achieving your organizational goals. This is what informs our data-driven approach.

Our use of data-driven insights allows us to offer a comprehensive view of the leadership landscape. From candidate evaluations to market trends, we provide clear, quantitative data that supports every decision. This data enables you to understand the rationale behind each recommendation, whether it's the selection of a candidate or the proposed leadership strategy.

By leveraging analytics and insights, we give you a clearer understanding of how leadership choices align with your broader organizational goals. This enables you to make decisions that are not just intuitive but also backed by concrete, relevant data.

Throughout the process, we deliver comprehensive reports that summarize key findings and outcomes. These reports include analysis of candidate profiles, leadership gaps, cultural fit assessments, and other relevant metrics to ensure you evaluate progress in real-time. With each report, we highlight actionable recommendations that keep you aligned with your strategic objectives. This ensures that every decision supports long-term growth, enhances organizational effectiveness, and fosters a culture of accountability.

Key Takeaways

- Every organization is unique, and we start by thoroughly understanding your challenges, goals, and culture, ensuring that our approach is customized to your needs.
- Innovex's discovery phase includes gathering insights from key stakeholders through interviews, surveys, and interactive sessions, which helps us to pinpoint specific challenges, leadership gaps, and opportunities for innovation.
- We ensure that leadership strategies are tightly aligned with your organization's vision for the future, which helps bridge the gap between strategic aspirations and execution.
- Innovex relies on a comprehensive, data-driven approach to recruitment, combining a strong network, cutting-edge assessment tools, and behavioral evaluations to identify candidates who are not only qualified but also fit your organization's culture and values.
- At Innovex, prioritize cultural alignment alongside technical skills to ensure that the selected leadership candidates can integrate seamlessly into your organization's existing culture and drive performance effectively.
- Through leadership coaching and retention planning, we

provide ongoing support to ensure that leaders continue to develop and thrive within your organization, driving sustainable growth.

5

Key Leadership Challenges: Identifying the Right Talent, Retention Strategies, and Strengthening Board Performance

We live in a highly competitive and dynamic business environment, where identifying and retaining the right talent ranks is one of the most pressing challenges for organizations. Data reveals that nearly 70% of leaders consider talent acquisition and retention a top priority, with the average cost of replacing a senior leader reaching 200% of their annual salary. These data show the great importance of the immense financial and operational impact of talent-related challenges on organizational success.

Identifying the Right Talent in a Competitive Market

Market saturation, globalization, and evolving employee expectations have created a complex and competitive landscape where the demand for skilled and adaptable leaders often outpaces the supply. However, identifying the "right" talent is more than just filling leadership roles; it's about aligning candidates with the organization's specific needs, culture, and long-term objectives. However, as an organization, you must define what the right talent means to you. This is because the concept of "right talent" varies across industries and roles. For example, companies in tech often look for leaders who excel in innovation, agile methodologies, and digital transformation, while those in healthcare focus on professionals with strong operational leadership skills and a commitment to patient care.

By clearly identifying what constitutes the "right talent" it gives you a focus on the kind of talent required and helps streamline your recruitment strategies.

Challenges in Attracting Leadership Talent

A major challenge in attracting leadership talent is market saturation. The pool of qualified leadership candidates is crowded, which makes it difficult for organizations to identify standout individuals. Also, there have been shortages in critical areas, such as digital leadership, which is worsening this challenge. Also, competing on a global scale adds layers of complexity, which entails creating an inclusive environment for different cultural differences and understanding and navigating varying regulations. Organizations must adopt a global mindset to attract talent from diverse regions to fill highly technical and specialized roles, and that may be challenging for startups and small organizations that are yet to establish a solid global presence.

Modern talents prioritize meaningful work, alignment with

values, and work-life balance over traditional perks. So, companies must adjust their offerings to meet these evolving priorities to attract these talents.

Strategies for Attracting and Identifying the Right Talent

Data-Driven Recruitment

Leverage technology and analytics to identify candidates with the right skills, potential, and cultural alignment. You can incorporate predictive analytics in the recruitment process, as it can help organizations predict a candidate's success by analyzing patterns in resumes, interviews, and performance data. Also, it helps streamline screening processes. Increase accuracy in identifying the leadership potential of the talents and reduce the recruitment cost. For instance, I worked with a multinational corporation that incorporated the use of AI-driven tools to identify mid-level managers capable of stepping into senior roles. By aligning historical performance data with leadership competencies, they were able to cut the time to fill senior positions by 30%.

Employer Branding

A compelling employer value proposition (EVP) is a magnet for top talent. This makes it challenging for smaller brands and techs to attract talent as talents are more aligned with the values and mission of organizations with strong brands. To combat this, you must focus on building a strong EVP. This includes:

- Clearly highlight the company's mission, vision, and culture.
- Share success stories that showcase growth opportunities of talents in your organizations.
- Promote a positive workplace culture through online platforms and employee testimonials.

By sharing the tangible impact of leadership decisions, such as innovation, work-life balance, supporting wellness and emphasis on employee growth, you tend to inspire the right talent. You have to state what you want your company to be known for and your branding strategies should be geared towards realizing that.

Networking and Referrals

Harnessing professional networks is a powerful way to uncover hidden talent. Many high-caliber candidates are passive job seekers and may only be accessible through referrals or networking. One of the best ways to go about this involves hosting industry events or webinars to connect with potential candidates, leveraging your professional networks for recommendations and maintaining alumni programs to engage with former employees. Also, you can incentivize employees to refer candidates by offering rewards for successful placements. This not only engages employees but also strengthens the talent pool.

Strategic Partnerships

Collaborating with executive search firms, leadership development organizations, and academic institutions can help access niche talent pools. This is a valuable route to consider if you require highly specialized expertise. The benefit of adopting this route is that it offers you access to access to previously vetted candidates, who have expertise in navigating industry-specific challenges.

Structured Interviews

Structured interviews entail standardizing the evaluation process to ensure that candidates are assessed consistently based on predefined competencies and organizational goals. To implement structured interviews, here are what to do:

- Define key competencies for the role, such as strategic thinking or adaptability.
- Develop role-specific scenarios to evaluate problem-solving skills.
- Use scoring rubrics for objective comparison.

Sample Question: "Describe a time when you led a team through a significant challenge. What was your strategy, and what were the results?"

Embracing Innovation in Talent Acquisition

We live in a global world where you have access to a global pool of talents; as such, it is possible to be in the US and locate a potential talent in Australia and interview without them having to leave the country. With the rise of remote work, you can cast a wider net by incorporating virtual hiring practices. You can get talents from different countries and regions to work remotely, and you can also facilitate their migration to the location of your organization after they have passed the digital interview process. The significance of embracing innovation in talent acquisition is that it prevents you from being limited. Adopt the use of storytelling in job postings to highlight organizational achievements and the role's potential for impact.

Retention Strategies for High-Performing Leaders

Retention of high-performing leaders is essential in maintaining organizational growth, stability, and innovation. While competitive compensation and benefits remain essential, organizations must go beyond financial incentives to create a compelling retention framework that resonates with their needs, values, and aspirations. They must develop a holistic approach to create an environment where leaders thrive. Here are the strategies to implement:

Transparent Communication

Open and honest communication about the organization's vision, goals, and challenges helps the leaders to understand the direction in which the organization is aiming, and this compels trust and dedication.

You must understand that transparency builds credibility and ensures alignment between leaders' efforts and the organization's strategic objectives. High-performing employees value clarity and inclusion in decision-making, as it enhances their commitment to the organization. When employees feel informed, they are more likely to invest their efforts into achieving shared goals.

For instance, you can host quarterly "Leadership Forums" where senior leaders discuss market trends, organizational challenges, and strategic priorities. The importance of such a forum is that it keeps leaders aligned with the company's direction and creates a shared sense of purpose.

Personalized Development Plans

Tailored growth opportunities, such as executive coaching, leadership training, and rotational assignments, play significant roles in keeping leaders engaged and motivated. It creates a culture of growth, which ensures that leaders remain both skilled and invested in the company's success.

Why this works is that high-performing leaders seek continuous learning and professional growth. Personalized development plans help leaders refine their skills, adapt to new challenges, and stay ahead in a competitive landscape. Such initiatives also demonstrate the organization's investment in its growth, which enhances its loyalty and commitment.

Equity Incentives

This is an effective retention strategy that works for startups. Performance-linked incentives and long-term equity options create a sense of ownership, which keeps the employee committed to the goal of the organization; as such, they are less likely to leave. Equity incentives entail providing leaders with a tangible stake in the company's growth and profitability. By linking rewards to performance outcomes, organizations create a sense of loyalty and ownership, which makes employees highly invested in the organization. For example, a tech startup can offer stock options with vesting schedules tied to the company's growth and profitability. This approach aligns leadership interests with the organization's trajectory and encourages long-term commitment.

Work-Life Integration

Flexible work arrangements and wellness programs address the holistic needs of employees and allow them to balance professional responsibilities with personal well-being. Organizations that prioritize this balance reduce burnout and increase job satisfaction, which helps to reduce the turnover rates of their employees. For instance, you can create a flexible schedule and wellness program that entails access to mental health resources, gym memberships, and wellness retreats. Also, you can provide support for family natives that entails offering on-site childcare, remote work options, and periodic wellness workshops. The importance of this is that it creates a culture of respect and support.

Proven Frameworks for Leadership Retention

To develop and implement effective retention strategies, organizations can draw on proven psychological and organizational frameworks. Below is a detailed explanation of three widely used frameworks, with specific steps on how to adopt each approach for talent retention.

The Employee Value Proposition (EVP) Framework

The EVP framework focuses on creating a comprehensive value proposition for leaders, covering five key areas: rewards, opportunities, organization, work environment, and people.

How It Works

- Rewards: Competitive salary, equity incentives, and comprehensive benefits attract and retain employees.
- Opportunities: Growth opportunities, challenging projects, and mentorship programs ensure professional fulfillment.
- Organization: A strong vision, culture, and positive reputation inspire leaders to remain committed.
- Work Environment: Flexible work arrangements, diversity initiatives, and inclusion promote satisfaction.
- People: Collaboration with supportive and inspiring colleagues strengthens the bond between leaders and the organization.

Steps to Adopt

- Organize workshops or surveys to identify leadership priorities across the five EVP areas.
- Create tailored compensation packages, including performance-linked bonuses or equity incentives.
- Offer flexible work arrangements, such as hybrid models or sabbaticals, to meet leaders' needs for work-life integration.

Facilitate leadership collaboration through retreats, team-building activities, or cross-functional projects.

Maslow's Hierarchy of Needs (Applied to Leadership Retention)

Maslow's framework emphasizes fulfilling various levels of human needs, which can be directly applied to employee retention. Addressing these needs ensures leaders feel secure, valued, and motivated to contribute to organizational success.

How It Works

- Physiological and Safety Needs: Employees require competitive compensation, comprehensive benefits, and job security. Without these essentials, dissatisfaction and disengagement can arise.
- Belongingness and Esteem Needs: Recognizing achievements, promoting inclusion, and creating a sense of community satisfy these needs. Employees tend to thrive in an environment that values their contributions and

strengthens their professional relationships.
- Self-Actualization: Providing opportunities for innovation, leadership development, and meaningful work helps employee achieve their fullest potential, which drives engagement and retention.

Steps to Adopt

- Conduct regular compensation and benefits reviews to ensure alignment with industry standards.
- Implement recognition programs that celebrate employee achievements, such as awards or public acknowledgments.
- Provide access to growth opportunities like executive training, innovation initiatives, or involvement in strategic projects.

Herzberg's Two-Factor Theory

Herzberg's theory categorizes workplace factors into two groups: hygiene factors and motivators. Addressing both is critical for retaining top leadership talent.

How It Works

- Hygiene Factors: Prevent dissatisfaction by ensuring fair pay, effective policies, job security, and a positive physical and cultural work environment. While these factors may not increase motivation, their absence leads to dissatisfaction.
- Motivators: Drive satisfaction by providing meaningful work, opportunities for achievement, recognition, and

professional growth.

Steps to Adopt

- Conduct surveys to identify gaps in hygiene factors, such as inadequate compensation or outdated policies.
- Invest in creating a positive work environment, including modernized facilities and tools for employees.
- Develop motivator programs, such as mentorship opportunities, leadership workshops, and personalized career pathways.

Practical Insights for Adoption

1. Data-Driven Customization: Use surveys, focus groups, and one-on-one discussions to gather employee-specific insights. Tailor retention strategies based on this feedback to maximize impact.
2. Continuous Feedback Loops: Regularly evaluate the effectiveness of implemented strategies. Adjust programs to reflect evolving leadership needs and market trends.
3. Integration with Organizational Goals: Align retention strategies with broader organizational objectives. This ensures that leadership efforts are contributing directly to long-term success.
4. Cultural Alignment: Build a company culture that reflects core values, promoting authenticity and a sense of belonging for employees.

Enhancing Board Performance

Boards of directors are instrumental in guiding organizations toward long-term success, ensuring strategic oversight, and promoting accountability. They are responsible for critical decisions that influence the direction and growth of companies. However, despite their importance, achieving high board performance is often a complex and challenging endeavor. Persistent issues such as misalignment, lack of diversity, and unclear roles can significantly hinder the board's effectiveness.

In my experience as the founder of Innovex, I have worked closely with various organizations to address these challenges. In one notable case, I helped a global financial services firm overhaul a stagnant board that was struggling with decision-making and alignment. The transformation of this board into a high-performing team provides an insightful example of how companies can strategically enhance board performance.

Key Factors Impacting Board Performance

Clear Role Definition

One of the foremost factors contributing to ineffective board performance is a lack of clear role definition. When board members are uncertain of their responsibilities, the entire board dynamic suffers. This confusion can lead to inefficiencies, overlap in duties, and a lack of accountability. To avoid such pitfalls, organizations must establish unambiguous roles and responsibilities for each board member. This clarity helps to streamline decision-making, facilitates effective communication, and ensures that each member contributes to the strategic direction of the company.

In the case of the global financial services firm I mentioned, one of the first steps was to redefine the roles of board members. I worked closely with the CEO and the board to identify the gaps in leadership and expertise that were affecting the company's ability to make informed and timely decisions. We created clear role descriptions for each board member, ensuring that their skills, experience, and personal strengths aligned with the company's strategic goals. This helped to resolve confusion, empower individual board members, and create greater accountability within the group.

Board Diversity

Diversity is another crucial factor for enhancing board performance. When boards lack diversity in terms of skills, experience, gender, and cultural background, they are at risk of making decisions that are narrow in scope and fail to consider a variety of perspectives. Diverse boards are better equipped to think creatively, adapt to change, and make informed decisions that reflect a broader range of viewpoints. Moreover, a diverse board promotes inclusivity and signals to the broader market that the organization values a range of perspectives.

In the case of the financial services firm, a significant part of the restructuring effort involved diversifying the board to ensure that it represented a wider array of skills and backgrounds. The previous board had been comprised of individuals with similar professional experiences, which limited the board's ability to consider innovative solutions and adapt to emerging trends in the financial services industry. By broadening the recruitment process to include individuals with diverse professional backgrounds, gender, and cultural perspectives, the board was able to make more strategic, inclusive decisions. This diversity became a key driver in the board's increased effectiveness and organizational performance.

Continuous Education

Boards must continually adapt to the changing business landscape to remain effective. This includes staying updated on industry trends, emerging technologies, and best practices in governance. Continuous education is essential for board members to make informed decisions, provide valuable insights, and lead the organization with a forward-thinking mindset.

In the case of the financial services firm, I facilitated ongoing training sessions for the board. These sessions were focused on the latest trends in governance, technological advancements, and changes in the financial sector that could impact the company's strategy. The training also included insights on governance best practices, which empowered the board to make more strategic, informed decisions. This investment helped the board to gain confidence in their roles which influenced their performance.

Regular Performance Evaluations

To enhance board performance, it is vital to conduct regular performance evaluations. These evaluations provide an opportunity to assess individual and collective effectiveness, identify areas for improvement, and celebrate successes. Performance assessments also allow for constructive feedback, which can be used to adjust strategies, realign goals, and optimize board dynamics.

For the financial services firm, regular performance evaluations were implemented as part of the restructuring process. The board conducted annual assessments to review its effectiveness in key areas such as governance, strategy, and cultural alignment. These evaluations were based on clear metrics. Over time, these evaluations helped the board fine-tune its strategies and decision-making processes, contributing to a 15% increase in the company's organizational performance within a year.

Problem Identification and Solution Implementation

In situations where the board is under performing, to enhance the performance, you have to first identify the issue or underlying cause of the under performance and inefficiencies. It could be anything from communication problems between the board members to unskilled board members.

In the case of when board members are not communicating effectively, you will have to devise a problem to solve the situation. When your board members in your organization do not have good communication, it will definitely impact the organization's performance. When there is no proper communication, there is no proper alignment of goals.

Facilitate a series of workshops to improve communication and resolve conflict. In such workshops, allow board members to discuss their perspectives. From these discussions, you will be able to identify the concerns and realign their goals with the broader strategic vision of the company.

Conversely, board members are lacking in areas such as technology, digital transformation, and diversity of thought. There are two ways to go about it. It can be through facilitating training to train the board members in specific skills or recruit professionals to fill in relevant spaces in the board.

There is no one right approach. The right approach is dependent on the nature of the board, its current state and the organizational goal. I've never had to adopt the same strategy when consulting for clients with board performance issues. I do use the same concept at times, but the mode of implementation and the specific strategies are usually unique. This is because no two organizations have the exact type and dynamics of the board.

To ensure the board remained aligned with the company's goals, implement quarterly strategy workshops focused on high-level discussions regarding the company's vision, strategic priorities, and emerging market trends. By encouraging open dialogue and brainstorming, the board will be able to develop a more cohesive strategy that helps drive the company's growth.

Case Study: Discover How Innovex Helps Retain Talent During a Leadership Transition

One of my most rewarding experiences was guiding a high-growth tech company through a critical founder-to-CEO transition. This period of change brought heightened uncertainty and the risk of losing key leaders—a scenario that could jeopardize the company's strategic goals and stability.

Recognizing the stakes, I designed and implemented a comprehensive retention strategy that addressed the leadership team's concerns and motivations:

- Transparent Communication: Regular updates and open discussions fostered trust and aligned expectations.
- Personalized Development Plans: Customized growth paths aligned with organizational needs with individual aspirations.
- Equity Incentives: Stock options encouraged long-term commitment and a sense of ownership.

Outcome

The results were transformative. 90% of the leadership team remained, ensuring operational continuity and a seamless transition. This success not only validated the importance of strategic retention investments but also demonstrated the value of a tailored approach to leadership challenges.

Key Takeaways

- Nearly 70% of leaders prioritize talent acquisition and retention due to the high costs of replacing senior leaders.
- It's essential to understand what the right talent means for your organization, which varies by industry and role.
- Market saturation, global competition, and evolving employee expectations complicate the recruitment of leadership talent.
- Leverage technology, analytics, and AI tools to streamline recruitment and improve hiring accuracy, reducing time and costs.
- A strong employer value proposition (EVP) helps attract top talent by emphasizing company culture, growth opportunities, and mission alignment.
- Building professional networks and incentivizing employee referrals are key strategies for uncovering high-quality candidates.
- Collaborate with executive search firms, educational institutions, and leadership development organizations to access niche talent pools.
- Transparent communication, personalized development plans, and work-life integration are essential for retaining high-performing leaders.
- Offering stock options or performance-linked incentives creates a sense of ownership, improving leader retention and commitment.
- Implement frameworks like EVP, Maslow's Hierarchy, and Herzberg's Two-Factor Theory to address both hygiene factors and motivators for leadership retention.

6

Frameworks and Strategies for Success: Building High-Impact Leadership Teams and Effective Boards

In my experience as the founder of Innovex working with several organizations, for a leadership team to be high impact, there are key elements that must be in place. This goes too for creating cohesive boards and retaining top talent. Also, models like the McKinsey 7-S Framework, Tuckman's Stages of Team Development, and Kotter's 8-Step Change Model have helped me in developing strategies, all of which I've integrated into my approach to leadership development and organizational transformation.

In this chapter, we will look at what building a high-impact leadership team entails, ways you can create a cohesive and effective board and how to implement these frameworks in delivering targeted results in your company.

Defining a High-Impact Leadership Team

A high-impact leadership team is a foundational component of organizational success. These teams comprise visionary, skilled, and collaborative leaders who work in unison to align the organization's goals with its mission and values. They transcend traditional leadership by building an environment of innovation, adaptability, and empowerment, enabling their teams to perform at their peak. Also, a high-impact leadership team can navigate complex challenges, make data-driven decisions, and deliver measurable results that contribute to sustainable growth and long-term value for stakeholders.

To understand what sets high-impact leadership teams apart, it's essential to examine their defining characteristics and how these traits drive success.

Key Characteristics of High-Impact Leadership Teams

Strong Alignment with Organizational Vision and Values

High-impact leadership teams have a deep understanding of their organization's vision and values. This alignment ensures that their strategic decisions and actions are always anchored in the broader mission of the organization. Leaders in such teams continuously communicate and reinforce these values across all levels of the organization to ensure the team employees are constantly connected with the organizational values.

For example, a team leading an environmentally conscious company ensures that every initiative, from product development to marketing, reflects its commitment to sustainability.

How to Foster Alignment:

- Clearly articulate the organization's mission, vision, and values.
- Develop leadership strategies that integrate these principles into daily operations.
- Regularly revisit and refine these values to ensure they remain relevant in a changing market.

A Balance of Diverse Skills, Expertise, and Perspectives

Diversity is a critical factor in creating a high-impact leadership team. For your team to be high-impact, it should comprise individuals with varied professional backgrounds, expertise, and problem-solving approaches. Diversity fuels creativity, innovation, and adaptability, which enables organizations to address challenges from multiple angles and seize opportunities in dynamic environments.

For instance, a team that combines technical expertise, strategic acumen, and cultural intelligence is better equipped to navigate international markets or implement complex technologies. This diversity fosters holistic decision-making, reduces blind spots, and mitigates risks.

How to Cultivate Diversity:

- Recruit leaders with complementary skill sets and experiences.

- Promote inclusivity by ensuring representation across gender, ethnicity, age, and professional backgrounds.
- Encourage open discussions where all perspectives are valued and considered.
- Create a system of no discrimination between employees and stakeholders.

Exceptional Communication and Decision-Making Capabilities

Communication is the lifeline of a high-impact leadership team. A defining feature of high-impact leaders is that they allow for free communication between each other, their teams, and external stakeholders. Transparent and open communication builds trust, resolves conflicts, and ensures that everyone is aligned on priorities and objectives.

Moreover, high-impact leaders excel in decision-making. They rely on data-driven insights, collaborative discussions, and strategic thinking to arrive at informed decisions that advance the organization's goals. They balance short-term wins with long-term impacts, ensuring their actions are sustainable and beneficial.

How to Enhance Communication and Decision-Making:

- Use collaborative tools and platforms to streamline communication across teams.
- Encourage active listening to understand different viewpoints.
- Leverage data analytics and scenario planning to guide

decision-making processes.

A Culture of Trust, Accountability, and Continuous Learning

Trust and accountability are the foundational basis of effective leadership teams. Trust isn't bought but earned. As a high-impact leader, you should earn the trust of your team members by being transparent, ethical, and consistent in their actions. Also, hold themselves and others accountable for delivering results, ensuring that everyone contributes to the organization's success.

In addition, these teams embrace a culture of continuous learning. They invest in leadership development, stay updated on industry trends, and adapt to changes in the market. This commitment to learning ensures they remain competitive and capable of addressing emerging challenges.

How to Build a Culture of Trust, Accountability, and Learning:

- Set clear expectations and follow through on commitments.
- Provide constructive feedback and celebrate achievements.
- Offer ongoing professional development opportunities, such as workshops, mentoring, and online courses.

The Role of High-Impact Leadership Teams in Driving Organizational Success

Enhancing Organizational Performance

High-impact leadership teams directly influence the overall performance of an organization. Their ability to align goals, communicate effectively, and make informed decisions ensures that resources are utilized efficiently and strategically. By fostering collaboration and innovation, these teams unlock potential across the organization, driving higher productivity and achieving key performance indicators (KPIs).

For example, a leadership team at a technology company may work together to streamline product development cycles, implement agile methodologies, and improve time-to-market. This alignment of goals and execution leads to enhanced organizational performance and competitive advantage.

Navigating Change and Uncertainty

The business landscape is rapidly changing, and this has made adaptability a crucial trait for survival and thriving. High-impact leadership teams are equipped to lead organizations through periods of uncertainty, such as economic downturns, technological disruptions, or regulatory changes. They have been taught to remain focused on the organization's mission while finding innovative solutions to navigate these challenges.

Such leadership teams are proactive in identifying potential risks and opportunities, using scenario planning and contingency strategies to remain resilient in the face of adversity.

Empowering Employees and Building a Positive Culture

A key role of high-impact leadership teams is to empower employees by building an inclusive and supportive work environment. When employees feel valued and heard, they are more likely to perform at their best and remain committed to the organization. High-impact leaders also set the tone for organizational culture, promoting values like collaboration, integrity, and innovation. For instance, you can implement policies that prioritize employee well-being, such as flexible work arrangements or professional development programs. These initiatives not only enhance employee satisfaction but also contribute to higher retention rates and organizational success.

Steps to Build a High-Impact Leadership Team

To cultivate a high-impact leadership team for your organization, here are the strategies to follow:

1. Identify Leadership Needs: Assess the organization's current and future leadership requirements based on its strategic goals and outline them.
2. Recruit and Develop Talent: Hire leaders who align with the organization's values and possess the necessary skills and expertise. To ensure they are always updated on the recent happenings in the industry and the business world, invest in their continuous development through training, mentoring, and leadership programs.
3. Foster Collaboration: Create opportunities for leaders to collaborate across departments, encouraging cross-

functional teamwork and innovation.

4. Establish Metrics for Success: Define clear performance metrics for leadership teams and regularly review their progress to ensure alignment with organizational goals.

5. Promote Leadership Accountability: Encourage leaders to take ownership of their actions and decisions and create a system where leaders report their progress and responsibilities. It could be monthly or quarterly.

Creating Cohesive and Effective Boards

Cohesive and effective boards are indispensable to the success of any organization. They provide the strategic direction, oversight, and governance needed to ensure that the organization remains on course to achieve its mission. While each member brings unique expertise and insights, a board must function as a unified entity to drive meaningful and sustainable results.

Building such a board requires deliberate effort and strategic planning. The following steps outline how organizations can create cohesive and effective boards:

Establish Clear Roles and Expectations

One of the first steps in creating an effective board is defining the roles and responsibilities of its members. This includes distinguishing between governance duties and operational tasks to avoid overlaps or inefficiencies. Board members should focus on strategic oversight, policy-making, and long-term planning while leaving day-to-day operations to the executive team.

Best Practices for Clarity in Roles:

- Develop a clear governance framework that outlines responsibilities.
- Provide job descriptions for board members, detailing expected contributions and time commitments.
- Hold orientation sessions for new members to familiarize them with their roles and the organization's goals.

Establishing these boundaries ensures that board members can effectively fulfill their governance responsibilities without micromanaging operational tasks. This clarity minimizes conflicts and ensures the board operates efficiently.

Foster Diversity and Inclusion

Diversity is a key factor in creating a well-rounded and innovative board. A diverse board leverages different perspectives, skill sets, and experiences, enabling more comprehensive decision-making. Inclusion ensures that every board member feels valued and empowered to contribute.

Strategies for Promoting Diversity:

- Recruit members from various professional, cultural, and demographic backgrounds.
- Prioritize expertise in key areas such as finance, technology, legal, and marketing to address emerging organizational needs.
- Encourage gender, age, and ethnic diversity to reflect the communities or markets the organization serves.

Diversity goes beyond optics; it drives innovation and reduces groupthink by incorporating a variety of viewpoints in discussions and decision-making processes.

Encourage Open Communication

Effective boards thrive on transparent, respectful, and constructive communication. Creating a culture of openness allows members to voice their opinions, raise concerns, and engage in healthy debates without fear of judgment or retaliation.

How to Foster Open Communication:

- Use structured agendas for board meetings to ensure all critical topics are addressed.
- Implement rules that encourage equal participation and discourage domination by a few voices.
- Conduct regular one-on-one sessions between board members and the chairperson to address any concerns.

Open communication also extends to interactions between the board and the executive team. Regular updates, candid discussions, and mutual respect lay the foundation for strong collaboration.

Conduct Regular Evaluations

Assessing the board's performance is essential for maintaining its effectiveness. Evaluations help identify strengths, address weaknesses, and ensure the board remains aligned with the organization's objectives.

Approaches to Board Evaluations:

- Perform annual self-assessments where members evaluate their contributions and the board's overall performance.
- Seek feedback from the executive team on how well the board is supporting organizational goals.
- Use external facilitators to conduct impartial reviews and recommend improvements.

Regular evaluations ensure accountability and continuous improvement, which strengthens the board's role as a strategic asset.

Invest in Board Development

To remain effective, board members must stay informed about emerging trends, industry developments, and best practices in governance. Continuous learning equips them with the knowledge and skills needed to address evolving challenges.

Ways to Support Board Development:

- Organize training sessions on topics like governance, risk management, and compliance.
- Provide access to industry reports, white papers, and expert speakers.
- Encourage participation in professional conferences and networking events.

Key Takeaway

- High-Impact Leadership Teams Drive Success: These teams are visionary, skilled, and collaborative, aligning their actions with the organization's mission and values to achieve sustainable growth.
- Diversity Fuels Innovation: A balance of diverse skills, backgrounds, and perspectives within the leadership team enhances creativity and enables holistic decision-making.
- Communication & Decision-Making: Open, transparent communication and data-driven decision-making are essential for high-impact teams, fostering trust and alignment.
- Trust, Accountability & Continuous Learning: Cultivating a culture of trust, holding team members accountable, and investing in ongoing learning ensure long-term success.
- Enhancing Organizational Performance: High-impact teams boost performance by aligning goals, improving collaboration, and driving productivity.
- Navigating Change with Adaptability: These teams can lead organizations through uncertainty, proactively managing risks and seizing opportunities.
- Empowering Employees: High-impact leadership teams build inclusive environments where employees feel valued, leading to higher satisfaction and retention.
- Clear Leadership Metrics: Establishing clear performance metrics and reviewing progress regularly ensures alignment with organizational goals.
- Creating Cohesive Boards: Successful boards require clear roles, diversity, open communication, and regular evaluations to function effectively and support organizational

success.

- Investing in Board Development: Continuous learning and development opportunities for board members help them stay informed and effective in their governance roles.

7

Practical Strategies for Retaining Top Talent Through Engagement

Retaining top talent is one of the most critical challenges organizations face today. High turnover disrupts operations and increases costs related to recruitment, onboarding, and training.

In my years of experience, engagement is one of the major keys to retention; when employees feel valued, supported, and connected to the organization's mission, they are more likely to stay and contribute at their best.

Here are the following proven strategies that outline how organizations can retain top talent by fostering engagement:

Offer Growth Opportunities

Employees who perceive a clear path for growth within the organization are more likely to remain committed. Professional development programs, cross-functional projects, and mentorship opportunities provide avenues for personal and career advancement. It lets the employees know that the organization values their contributions and is committed to their success, which every employee desires.

How to Create Growth Opportunities:

- Establish career progression frameworks with transparent criteria for promotions.
- Provide access to training programs, certifications, and tuition reimbursement.
- Assign high-potential employees to challenging projects that expand their skill sets.

Recognize and Reward Contributions

Recognition is a powerful motivator that reinforces positive behavior and performance. Employees who feel acknowledged for their efforts are more engaged and loyal to the organization. Make the recognition programs inclusive and equitable, ensuring all employees have an opportunity to be celebrated for their contributions.

Ideas for Recognition and Rewards:

- Implement a formal recognition program with awards for exceptional performance.
- Celebrate achievements publicly during team meetings or events.
- Offer both monetary rewards (bonuses, salary increases) and non-monetary incentives (extra time off, personalized thank-you notes).

Foster a Culture of Feedback

Regular feedback helps employees understand how their work aligns with organizational goals and where they can improve. It also creates a platform for employees to voice their concerns and ideas. Furthermore, it helps build trust and strengthens the relationship between employees and leadership.

How to Build a Feedback Culture:

- Conduct frequent one-on-one meetings between employees and managers.
- Use 360-degree feedback systems to gather input from peers, subordinates, and supervisors.
- Act on feedback by addressing concerns and implementing viable suggestions.

Prioritize Well-Being

Organizations that prioritize employee well-being create an environment where individuals can thrive both professionally and personally. Supporting physical, mental, and emotional health is essential for sustaining engagement. Employees who feel their well-being is valued are more likely to stay committed to their organization. This is a major reason why many employees prioritize organizations that emphasize wellness and work-life balance.

Well-Being Initiatives to Consider:

- Offer flexible work arrangements, such as remote work or compressed workweeks.
- Provide wellness programs, including fitness classes, mind-

fulness workshops, and access to mental health resources.
- Encourage work-life balance by discouraging after-hours communication and promoting regular vacations.

Enhance Workplace Communication

Transparency is a vital component of employee engagement. Keeping employees informed about organizational changes, strategies, and goals fosters a sense of trust and involvement. When employees are well-informed, they feel empowered to contribute to organizational success, and this increases their sense of purpose and loyalty.

Tips for Improving Communication:

- Use town halls, newsletters, and team meetings to share updates and celebrate successes.
- Encourage managers to maintain open-door policies, making themselves accessible to employees.
- Leverage technology platforms to streamline communication and collaboration.

Frameworks and Models for Success

Achieving organizational success requires well-defined frameworks and models that guide strategy, execution, and continuous improvement. Frameworks serve as structured approaches that organizations can use to assess, realign, and enhance performance while adapting to market dynamics and challenges.

Three highly effective and widely adopted frameworks are the McKinsey 7-S Framework, Tuckman's Stages of Team Development and Kotter's 8-Step Change Model, which emphasizes the interdependence of critical organizational elements.

McKinsey 7-S Framework

The McKinsey 7-S Framework is a strategic management tool designed to assess and enhance organizational effectiveness. Developed by McKinsey & Company, it emphasizes the importance of aligning seven interdependent elements to drive performance and achieve business goals. By analyzing these components, organizations can identify strengths, address misalignments, and create a cohesive environment that supports long-term success. This framework is particularly useful for organizational change, performance improvement, and strategic planning.

Key Elements of the McKinsey 7-S Framework

1. **Strategy:** A clear and actionable plan that defines how the organization achieves its goals and maintains a competitive edge. For example, it can be to dominate the AI market through innovation and partnerships as a tech company.
2. **Structure:** The organizational design includes hierarchy, reporting relationships, and communication flow. For instance, a flat structure in a startup promotes collaboration and rapid decision-making.
3. **Systems:** This refers to processes and procedures that drive daily operations and decision-making. For example, a robust CRM system that enhances customer relationship management and streamlines sales.
4. **Shared Values:** The core beliefs and cultural principles that

shape organizational identity and decision-making. For example, a sustainability-driven company will prioritize environmentally friendly practices.

5. **Style:**This refers to leadership style and organizational culture. It could be transformation, authoritarian, or laissez-faire leadership.
6. **Staff:**This refers to people within the organization, including their roles, capabilities, and engagement levels.
7. **Skills:**The collective competencies and expertise within the organization.

Application of the McKinsey 7-S Framework

The McKinsey 7-S Framework can be applied in various contexts to drive organizational success. Let's look at some practical ways you can leverage this framework:

1. **Internal Alignment:** Identify and correct mismatches between strategy, structure, and systems to improve efficiency. This entails identifying inconsistencies, aligning shared values with policies and adjust staff roles and skills
2. **Leadership Evaluation:** Assess leadership style and skills to ensure they support organizational goals. Also, address skill gaps with training
3. **Optimizing Systems & Processes:** Ensure **systems** support strategic objectives for efficiency. This entails identifying inefficiencies, implementing advanced tools and monitoring system performance

Tuckman's Stages of Team Development

Dr. Bruce Tuckman's model outlines five stages that teams go through as they evolve: Forming, Storming, Norming, Performing, and Adjourning. Each stage describes the team's progression from initial formation to achieving optimal performance and eventually disbanding. Understanding these stages helps leaders to build strong team dynamics and ensure seamless transitions.

The Five Stages of Team Development

1. **Forming:**The team comes together, with members focusing on getting to know each other and understanding their roles. This stage often involves high levels of uncertainty and reliance on leadership for direction. For example, when onboarding a new leadership team, provide a clear overview of responsibilities, the organization's mission, and expected outcomes to build a solid foundation.
2. **Storming:**This is the most challenging stage, as differences in opinions, working styles, and priorities may lead to conflicts. However, addressing these challenges early fosters growth and mutual understanding. Create an opportunity for open communication, mediate disputes, and establish ground rules for collaboration. As a leader in the organization, you can host conflict-resolution workshops or facilitate discussions to align perspectives.
3. **Norming:**The team begins to establish trust and cohesion. Members align around shared goals, and collaboration becomes more seamless. You can continually reinforce team unity by celebrating milestones, fostering mutual

respect, and ensuring that everyone's contributions are acknowledged.

4. **Performing:**At this stage, the team achieves peak efficiency and productivity. Members work independently while contributing to the group's success. Also, empower the team by providing resources, encouraging innovation, and offering constructive feedback.

5. **Adjourning:**Teams disband after achieving their objectives. This stage requires leaders to ensure smooth transitions and provide opportunities for reflection and recognition.

Application of Tuckman's Model

Tuckman's model provides actionable insights for leaders looking to build and manage effective teams. Below are practical ways to apply this framework:

1. **Clarifying Roles and Expectations (Forming):** When new teams are formed, ambiguity about roles and responsibilities can lead to confusion. Leaders can use the Forming stage to set clear expectations.

2. **Navigating Conflict (Storming):** Conflicts are inevitable, but they can be constructive if managed effectively. Leaders can use the Storming stage to address underlying issues and foster collaboration.

3. **Building Trust and Cohesion (Norming):** Trust and cohesion are vital for team success. Leaders can focus on shared goals and celebrate small wins to foster unity.

4. **Encouraging Peak Performance (Performing):** During the Performing stage, leaders can empower teams by

providing autonomy and fostering innovation.

5. **Facilitating Smooth Transitions (Adjourning):** When teams disband, leaders should ensure a smooth transition by recognizing contributions and offering support. This entails organizing a formal farewell event for departing board members to acknowledge their impact and provide mentorship opportunities for successors.

Kotter's 8-Step Change Model

John Kotter's 8-Step Change Model is a road map for leading successful organizational change. It emphasizes the importance of creating a sense of urgency, building coalitions, and sustaining momentum to ensure lasting transformation.

The Eight Steps of Kotter's Model

1. **Create Urgency:** Highlight the need for change by communicating its importance and potential benefits.
2. **Build a Guiding Coalition:** Assemble a diverse group of leaders and influencers to champion the change initiative.
3. **Develop a Vision and Strategy:** Craft a clear vision and actionable strategy to guide the organization through change.
4. **Communicate the Vision:** Share the vision with stakeholders through transparent and consistent messaging.
5. **Empower Action:** Remove barriers and provide resources to enable employees to contribute to the change effort.
6. **Generate Short-Term Wins:** Celebrate early successes to build momentum and demonstrate the value of the change.
7. **Consolidate Gains and Drive More Change:** Use early wins

to drive further change and address lingering challenges.

8. **Anchor New Approaches in the Culture:** Embed the change into the organization's culture by aligning values, practices, and policies.

Application of Kotter's Model

Kotter's model is particularly effective for large-scale initiatives, such as leadership transitions, organizational restructuring, or digital transformation. Below are practical applications:

1. **Guiding Leadership Transitions:** Leadership changes can be disruptive, but Kotter's model provides a structured approach to managing the process. For instance, during a CEO transition, create a sense of urgency by communicating the need for new leadership to navigate market challenges.

2. **Ensuring Stakeholder Buy-In:** Change initiatives often face resistance, making stakeholder buy-in critical. Kotter's emphasis on vision communication helps overcome barriers. For instance, during a board restructuring, host regular meetings with stakeholders to address concerns and provide updates on progress.

3. **Sustaining Momentum:** Maintaining momentum is essential for long-term success. Kotter's focus on short-term wins and consolidating gains ensures continuous progress. To keep the momentum going, ensure to celebrate milestones as they help serve as a basis to inspire further innovation.

Visual Tools and Data Representation

Visual tools and data representation are essential for simplifying complex information, enhancing decision-making, and fostering strategic discussions. Here, we will explore three powerful tools—Leadership Pipeline Chart, Board Effectiveness Heat map, and Engagement Metrics Dashboard—that provide actionable insights.

Leadership Pipeline Chart

The Leadership Pipeline Chart visually represents how talent progresses within an organization, from entry-level roles to senior leadership positions. This tool helps identify gaps in leadership development and succession planning and ensures that there is a steady supply of qualified leaders.

Key Components of a Leadership Pipeline Chart

1. **Levels of Leadership:**

- Entry-Level Roles
- Mid-Level Management
- Senior Leadership
- Executive Roles

1. **Talent Flow:** Arrows or paths indicate movement between levels.
2. **Pipeline Gaps:** Highlight areas where talent is not advancing as expected.

Benefits

- Succession Planning: Identifies potential successors for critical roles and highlights areas requiring talent development.
- Leadership Development: Pinpoint stages where employees need additional training or support to progress.
- Diversity Insights: Reveals disparities in gender, ethnicity, or other diversity metrics across leadership levels.

Practical Application

Example: A manufacturing company may discover that only 30% of mid-level managers transition to senior leadership due to a lack of leadership training programs. Using the Leadership Pipeline Chart, the organization can design targeted development initiatives to bridge this gap.

Board Effectiveness Heatmap

The Board Effectiveness Heatmap uses color-coded visualizations to evaluate areas of strength and improvement within a board of directors. This tool fosters focused discussions and promotes accountability.

Key Features of a Board Effectiveness Heat map

1. **Assessment Areas:**

- Governance and Compliance
- Strategic Oversight

- Financial Expertise
- Diversity and Inclusion
- Decision-Making Effectiveness

1. **Color Coding:**

- Green: Strong performance
- Yellow: Moderate performance
- Red: Needs improvement

Benefits

- Focused Improvement: Helps to pinpoint areas that require attention and inform the board on areas to allocate resources effectively.
- Accountability: Encourages board members to take responsibility for specific areas.
- Transparency: Facilitates open and constructive discussions about performance.

Practical Application

Example: A nonprofit organization may find that its heat map shows strong governance and compliance but highlights weaknesses in financial expertise. This insight prompts the board to recruit members with a financial background to strengthen its capabilities.

Engagement Metrics Dashboard

An Engagement Metrics Dashboard tracks employee engagement using key metrics such as retention rates, satisfaction surveys, and participation in development programs. This tool provides real-time insights into employee well-being and organizational health.

Key Metrics

- Retention Rates: Measures employee turnover and identifies patterns across departments or demographics.
- Satisfaction Surveys: Aggregates employee feedback to gauge morale and identify areas for improvement.
- Participation Rates: Tracks employee involvement in training, wellness programs, and other initiatives.

Benefits

- Proactive Decision-Making: Identifies engagement issues before they lead to higher turnover or decreased productivity.
- Cultural Insights: Reveals how employees perceive the workplace environment and leadership.
- Performance Correlation: Links engagement metrics with productivity and business outcomes.

Practical Application

Example: A technology firm may use an Engagement Metrics Dashboard to monitor satisfaction scores during a major organizational change, ensuring that employees feel supported and valued throughout the transition.

Visual Representation and Technology

To maximize the effectiveness of these tools, organizations can leverage advanced visualization software such as Power BI, Tableau, or Microsoft Excel. These platforms enable the creation of interactive dashboards, charts, and heat maps, which allow stakeholders to drill down into specific data points and uncover actionable insights.

Key Takeaways

- Engagement is critical for retention: Employees are more likely to stay when they feel valued, supported, and aligned with the organization's mission.
- Offer growth opportunities: Providing clear career progression, professional development, and challenging projects helps retain top talent.
- Recognition and rewards drive loyalty: Acknowledging employees' contributions through both monetary and non-monetary rewards boosts engagement and retention.
- Foster a feedback culture: Regular feedback builds trust, helps employees align with goals, and opens a platform for them to voice concerns and ideas.
- Prioritize employee well-being: Promoting physical, men-

PRACTICAL STRATEGIES FOR RETAINING TOP TALENT THROUGH...

tal, and emotional health supports long-term engagement and loyalty.

- Enhance workplace communication: Open, transparent communication keeps employees informed and empowered, strengthening their connection to the organization.
- McKinsey 7-S Framework: A comprehensive model focusing on aligning strategy, structure, systems, shared values, style, staff, and skills for optimal organizational performance.
- Tuckman's Stages of Team Development: Understanding the five stages (Forming, Storming, Norming, Performing, and Adjourning) helps manage team dynamics effectively.
- Kotter's 8-Step Change Model: A road map for leading organizational change, emphasizing urgency, coalition building, vision creation, and anchoring new practices.
- Visual tools for decision-making: Tools like the Leadership Pipeline Chart and Engagement Metrics Dashboard help assess and drive organizational success through clear, actionable insights.

8

Real-World Case Studies: Lessons in Leadership Transformation Across Industries

In this chapter, we explore real-world case studies of leadership transformation projects undertaken by Innovex. Through these examples, you'll gain practical insights into how leadership strategies are applied across various industries, the challenges faced, and the key lessons learned. Each case study highlights the unique way Innovex handle its tasks and jobs. Whether you're a business leader, entrepreneur, or aspiring change-maker, these lessons will equip you with the right knowledge to enhance your own leadership approach.

Case Study 1: Innovex Strategy in Transforming a Global Financial Firm's Stagnant Board into a High-Performing Team by 80%

A global financial services firm was facing a significant challenge: its board of directors was unable to make decisive strategic moves. The lack of cohesion among board members hindered the firm's ability to respond to market changes swiftly, which threatened its competitive advantage. The leadership of the firm struggled with misaligned priorities, inefficient communication, and slow decision-making processes, which created bottlenecks in implementing key initiatives. The firm's executive team recognized that without addressing these fundamental governance issues, the business's long-term sustainability and growth would be at risk.

Challenges Identified

Upon conducting a thorough analysis of the board's performance, several key issues were identified:

- Lack of Strategic Alignment: Board members had differing views on the company's vision and strategic direction, which led to inconsistent decision-making.
- Skill Gaps and Expertise Deficiency: The board lacked the necessary diversity in expertise. Expertise in critical areas such as risk management, technology, and global market expansion was lacking and underrepresented.
- Poor Governance and Accountability: There were unclear roles and responsibilities among board members, and that resulted in a lack of ownership and accountability.

- Ineffective Communication: Meetings were often unproductive. Their discussions are usually lengthy, with little actionable progress.
- Slow Decision-Making Processes: Due to the lack of trust and alignment, strategic decisions took longer than necessary, which delayed the execution of key business initiatives.

Solution Implemented

Recognizing the urgency of the situation, our team at Innovex developed and executed a multi-pronged intervention to revitalize the board's effectiveness. The following strategies were implemented:

Comprehensive Board Assessment

A detailed assessment was conducted to evaluate the existing board structure, identify competency gaps, and assess governance frameworks. This included:

- One-on-one interviews with board members and senior leaders.
- A skills matrix analysis to determine areas that needed strengthening.
- A review of past board meeting minutes to assess decision-making patterns.

Targeted Board Recruitment and Diversification

Based on the assessment findings, we implemented a targeted recruitment strategy to bring in new board members with diverse expertise in key areas such as digital transformation, regulatory compliance, and global finance. This ensured that the board had a balanced mix of skills, experience, and perspectives to drive informed strategic decisions.

Governance Enhancement and Role Clarity

To improve governance, we redefined the roles and responsibilities of board members, ensuring clear accountability. This included:

- Establishing new governance policies to streamline decision-making processes.
- Creating specialized committees (e.g., risk, audit, and strategy) to focus on critical areas.
- Implementing performance evaluation metrics for board effectiveness.

Strategy Workshops and Leadership Alignment

To ensure smooth collaboration and strategic cohesion in the management, we introduced regular workshops focused on:

- Aligning board members with the company's vision, mission, and long-term objectives.
- Enhancing decision-making agility through scenario planning and strategy simulations.

- Strengthening teamwork through executive coaching and leadership development sessions.

Improved Communication and Meeting Efficiency

To address communication challenges, new protocols were introduced, which are:

- Implementation of structured meeting agendas with clear objectives and time limits.
- Adoption of digital collaboration tools to facilitate real-time discussions and decision-making.
- Regular feedback loops between the board and executive leadership to ensure alignment.

Results Achieved

The transformation initiative yielded 80% improvements within a year. The board became more cohesive, with members working together towards common goals; as such, the decision-making process became more effective and faster. Furthermore, there was greater accountability, and specialized board committees enabled more focused and informed decision-making.

Key Lessons Learned

At Innovex, our proactive board management approach fosters leadership effectiveness and drives innovative solutions. By emphasizing diverse board composition, structured decision-making, clear accountability frameworks, and continuous leadership development, we ensure long-term organizational alignment and growth. Our commitment to efficient communication strengthens board collaboration, securing sustained strategic success.

Case Study 2: Retaining Talent During a Leadership Transition in a High-Growth Technology Company

A high-growth technology company was undergoing a critical leadership transition from a founder-led model to a new CEO. While the transition was strategically necessary to support the company's next phase of growth, it brought about significant uncertainty among senior leaders. Many key leaders who had been with the company since its inception had their loyalty tied to the founder's vision and leadership style.

The problem is that the company feared that it might lose key leaders, and this might lead to high employee turnover, disruption of ongoing projects, and a potential decline in innovation. Furthermore, external competitors were actively targeting the company's top talent, which created an urgent need to implement a robust retention strategy.

Challenges Identified

Several key issues emerged during the transition:

- Uncertainty and Lack of Trust: Employees, particularly leaders, were concerned about the new leadership's vision and how it would impact their roles and the company's future.

- Risk of Attrition: With multiple leaders receiving offers from competitors, the company faced the possibility of losing its top talent, and this, if allowed, will lead to knowledge gaps and operational inefficiencies.
- Engagement and Morale Issues: The leadership transition caused a decline in motivation among employees, and this greatly impacted their performance.
- Concerns Over Long-Term Growth Strategy: Leaders wanted clarity on how the new leadership would maintain the company's culture, innovation, and market position.

Solution Implemented

To address these challenges and ensure a smooth transition, we at Innovex developed a three-pronged approach focusing on communication, professional growth, and financial incentives.

Transparent Communication Strategy

To alleviate concern and build trust, there is a need for clear and consistent communication. Key actions included:

- Executive Town Halls: We guided the new CEO to hold multiple town halls and one-on-one meetings with key leaders to discuss the company's vision, strategy, and their roles in shaping the future.
- Regular Leadership Updates: We suggested a bi-weekly leadership newsletter to provide updates on the transition, business performance, and strategic goals to ensure that all leaders are well informed.
- Open-Door Policy: Leaders were encouraged to voice their

concerns and provide feedback directly to leadership.

Personalized Executive Development Plans

Retaining key leaders required more than just reassurance—it necessitated tangible career growth opportunities and appropriate remuneration. The following initiatives were introduced:

- Individual Growth Road-maps: Career development plans were created for each executive that clearly stated long-term growth opportunities, leadership training, and succession planning.
- Leadership Coaching: External leadership coaches were brought in to coach the leaders to adapt to the new leadership dynamics and align their personal career goals with the company's vision.
- Cross-Functional Projects: High-performing leaders were prompted to more strategic cross-functional head positions. Doing this helps to keep them challenged and engaged.

Equity and Incentive-Based Retention Program

Financial incentives play one of the top significant roles in retaining top talent. The company introduced the following measures:

- Equity Grants: To align executive interests with long-term company success, a new equity-based incentive program was introduced.
- Retention Bonuses: Performance-based retention bonuses

were offered to encourage the employee to remain in the company.

- Competitive Compensation Review: Salaries and benefits were Road-maps against industry standards to ensure competitiveness in the market.

Results Achieved

The implementation of these strategies yielded significant and measurable results:

- 90% Retention of Leadership Team: The vast majority of leaders remained with the company, ensuring continuity and stability during the transition.
- Seamless Transition with Minimal Disruption: Ongoing projects and innovation pipelines were not affected and this helped the company to maintain its competitive edge.
- Strengthened Executive Confidence and Engagement: Leaders became active champions of the new leadership, which kept their morale throughout the organization.

Key Lessons Learned

Innovex's structured executive search ensures leadership stability and sustained business growth through transparent processes, role-specific retention strategies, and competitive financial incentives.

Case Study 3: Innovex Approach in Improving Talent Acquisition at a FTSE Cybersecurity company

Our client, a global leader in cybersecurity, was facing challenges in its talent acquisition function. The company had ambitious growth plans, but its existing hiring processes, technology, and internal recruitment models were not equipped to scale efficiently. The lack of a structured and strategic approach to talent acquisition birthed a lot of inefficiencies, such as prolonged hiring cycles and difficulty in attracting top-tier talent.

They recognized the need to optimize its talent acquisition strategy to support business growth and maintain its competitive edge in the industry. To achieve this, the company partnered with Innovex to implement a comprehensive restructuring of its hiring processes.

Challenges Identified

Here are the key challenges that were uncovered during the initial assessment of the client's talent acquisition function:

- Inefficient Hiring Processes: The recruitment cycle was lengthy and inconsistent, and this led to a lot of delays in filling critical positions.
- Lack of Strategic Alignment: The talent acquisition function was not fully aligned with the company's business objectives, which made it difficult to identify and attract the right candidates.
- Outdated Technology Stack: Existing recruitment tools

and technology lacked automation and analytics, thereby making the hiring process stressful and cumbersome.

- Limited Internal Recruitment Capabilities: The internal recruitment team lacked a clear framework for sourcing, assessing, and engaging with candidates effectively.
- Difficulty in Attracting Top Talent: the client needed to enhance its employer brand and positioning to compete for the best talent in the cybersecurity industry.

Solution Implemented

Innovex designed and executed a multi-phase transformation plan to revamp the client's talent acquisition function. The focus was on optimizing processes, implementing the right technology, and improving internal recruitment models to ensure effectiveness.

Talent Acquisition Process Optimization

To streamline hiring, Innovex restructured the recruitment workflow and created a more structured and efficient approach to talent acquisition. Key initiatives that were implemented include:

- Standardizing recruitment processes across departments for consistency.
- Implementing structured interview frameworks to improve candidate evaluation.
- Reducing the time-to-hire by optimizing each stage of the recruitment cycle.

Implementation of Advanced Recruitment Technology

Innovex introduced a modern applicant tracking system (ATS) with automation and data analytics capabilities. This helped them to:

- Improve candidate sourcing and pipeline management.
- Automate administrative tasks, which allows recruiters to save time to focus on strategic hiring.
- Utilize data-driven insights to refine recruitment strategies and measure success.

Establishing a Robust Internal Recruitment Model

Innovex worked closely with the HR and leadership teams to create a sustainable internal recruitment framework. This included:

- Developing clear roles and responsibilities within the talent acquisition team.
- Training internal recruiters on best practices for sourcing and engagement.
- Building an internal talent pipeline to reduce reliance on external agencies.

Strategic Leadership Hiring

One of the key milestones of the transformation was the successful hiring of a Global Head of Talent Acquisition. This role was critical in driving the new strategy forward and ensuring alignment with the long-term business goals.

Enhancing Employer Brand and Talent Attraction

To position the business as an employer of choice in the cyber-security industry, Innovex developed a talent branding strategy that included:

- Revamping the company's career page and job descriptions to reflect its culture and values.
- Showcasing employee success stories to highlight career growth opportunities.
- Strengthening employer branding on social media and recruitment platforms.

Results Achieved

The transformation of the talent acquisition function delivered measurable improvements across key areas:

- 30% Significant Reduction in Time-to-Hire: Optimized processes led to a faster and more efficient recruitment cycle, which reduced hiring time by 30%.
- Successful Leadership Placement: The onboarding of a Global Head of Talent Acquisition provided strategic direction and leadership to the talent function.
- Improved Internal Recruitment Capabilities: The revamped internal hiring model reduced dependency on external recruiters, thereby helping the company to save costs by hiring over 1,000 directly in one year.
- Enhanced Candidate Experience: Structured processes and better technology created a seamless and positive experience for job applicants.

- Stronger Employer Brand: The improved talent branding initiatives increased the quality and volume of inbound applications.

Key Lessons Learned

Innovex's structured executive search ensures long-term leadership stability and business growth. A strategic approach to talent acquisition drives efficiency through process optimization, enhancing both hiring speed and quality. Technology is a game changer, enabling data-driven decisions and automating repetitive tasks for greater accuracy and efficiency. An effective in-house recruitment model reduces costs while improving long-term hiring outcomes. Furthermore, a strong talent brand attracts top-tier candidates, positioning Innovex as an industry leader in talent acquisition excellence.

Case Study 4: Innovex Strategic Executive Search for leading Ed-Tech Scale Up

A rapidly growing company, faced a critical need to strengthen its executive leadership team. With plans for expansion and increased market penetration in the Nordics, the company required seasoned professionals to drive revenue growth and operational success. To achieve this, the client engaged Innovex to lead executive searches for two key leadership roles: Chief Revenue Officer (CRO) and Country Manager for the Nordics.

Challenges Identified

The company's rapid expansion presented several recruitment challenges:

- Time-Sensitive Hiring Needs: The company needed to fill the roles quickly to maintain momentum in its growth strategy.
- Niche Talent Pool: Finding experienced candidates with the right mix of industry expertise, leadership skills, and market knowledge was challenging.
- Competitive Hiring Market: The Nordics' tech sector is highly competitive, which makes it difficult to attract top-tier executive talent.
- Alignment with Company Culture: Candidates had to fit into the client's innovative and high-performance culture while driving strategic initiatives.

Solution Implemented

Innovex deployed a structured and data-driven executive search strategy to identify and secure the right candidates for the client.

Executive Search Strategy Development

- We conducted in-depth consultations with the leadership team to define the ideal candidate profiles.
- Mapped out industry trends and competitor hiring practices to refine the search strategy.
- Established key performance indicators (KPIs) for the hir-

ing process to ensure alignment with business goals.

Targeted Talent Sourcing

- Leveraged Innovex's extensive executive talent network to source high—skilled candidates.
- Utilized AI-driven talent analytics to identify candidates with the right experience and leadership potential.
- Engaged in proactive outreach to top leaders in relevant industries across the Nordics.

Streamlined Selection and Assessment

- Designed a rigorous selection process, including behavioral interviews and competency-based assessments.
- Evaluated candidates based on leadership skills, cultural fit, and strategic vision.
- Conducted in-depth reference checks to validate candidates' past performance and leadership capabilities.

Efficient Hiring Process Execution

- Facilitated structured interviews and debrief sessions to ensure alignment among key stakeholders.
- Negotiated competitive compensation packages to secure top talent while maintaining budget efficiency.
- Provided on boarding support to ensure a smooth transition for the newly appointed leaders.

Results Achieved

The executive search process delivered significant benefits for the client:

- Successful Hiring of Key Leaders: Both the Chief Revenue Officer and the Country Manager for the Nordics were placed within the targeted time frame.
- Reduced the average hiring cycle by 30%: This helps save the company both time and resources.
- Enhanced Leadership Capabilities: The newly appointed leaders brought industry expertise and strategic vision, which is bun the race.
- Strengthened Market Presence: With strong leadership in place, the client accelerated its expansion and improved operational efficiency in the Nordics.

Key Lessons Learned

Innovex's structured executive search ensures long-term leadership stability and business growth through clear role definitions and data-driven talent sourcing that improve hiring outcomes. By prioritizing speed and precision in competitive hiring markets, Innovex leverages proactive outreach and streamlined assessments to minimize delays and secure top talent efficiently.

Case Study 5: Innovex Strengthening Leadership at leading Dutch Fintech Through Executive Search

Our client recognized its need to strengthen its executive leadership team to sustain growth and drive strategic initiatives. To achieve this, they partnered with Innovex to identify and secure top-tier executive talent for crucial leadership roles, including Chief Financial Officer (CFO), Chief Marketing Officer (CMO), and UK Managing Director (UK MD). In addition, Innovex continued to support the client's affiliated companies by delivering board-level talent.

Challenges Identified

The leadership expansion efforts faced several key challenges:

1. Critical Need for Executive Leadership: The company requires highly experienced leaders capable of managing the organization in this competitive business market.
2. Industry-Specific Expertise: Candidates need to possess a deep understanding of the industry and have a track record of success in similar roles.
3. Tight Hiring Timeline: The leadership positions needed to be filled within a strict time frame to ensure business continuity and strategic execution.
4. Cultural and Strategic Alignment: Leaders had to align with the client's corporate culture and long-term strategic vision.

Solution Implemented

Innovex deployed a structured executive search strategy to address these challenges and deliver strong leadership candidates.

Comprehensive Role Analysis and Talent Strategy

- Conducted in-depth consultations with the executive team to understand role requirements and long-term business goals.
- Mapped industry trends to identify key skills and experience necessary for success in the targeted roles.
- Developed an executive search framework with a focus on leadership, cultural alignment, and strategic impact.

Targeted Search and Candidate Engagement

- Leveraged Innovex's extensive executive network and talent intelligence platform to source high-caliber candidates.
- Engaged in proactive outreach to attract industry-leading professionals with proven success.
- Used data-driven assessment tools to shortlist candidates based on leadership capabilities, technical expertise, and cultural fit.

Rigorous Selection and Assessment Process

- Conducted structured interviews and leadership competency evaluations.
- Assessed candidates through scenario-based problem-solving exercises relevant to their business landscape.

- Performed thorough reference checks to validate past performance and leadership effectiveness.

Seamless Hiring and On boarding Support

- Facilitated structured negotiations and offer processes to secure top talent within budget and timelines needed.
- Provided onboarding support to ensure a smooth transition for newly appointed leaders.

Results Achieved

The strategic approach implemented by Innovex led to several impactful outcomes:

- Successful Placement of Key Leaders: Innovex secured high-skilled and qualified personnel for the CFO, CMO, and UK MD positions.
- 70% Enhanced Governance and Decision-Making: Innovex continued to place board-level talent in the client's affiliated companies, which ensured strong governance and strategic oversight.
- Accelerated Business Growth: With a reinforced leadership team, the client achieved greater market expansion and operational efficiency.

Key Lessons Learned

Innovex's structured executive search ensures long-term leadership stability and business growth by combining strategic, targeted search processes with speed and precision to secure top-tier talent efficiently. We prioritize cultural and strategic alignment to ensure leaders fit seamlessly within the organization, driving sustained impact. As a trusted talent partner, Innovex delivers ongoing leadership solutions that adapt to evolving business needs, fostering lasting success.

Case Study 6: Optimizing Executive Recruitment for B2C Health Technology business

A rapidly growing company in the healthcare and wellness sector, needs to strengthen its executive leadership team that will be capable of driving strategic initiatives and business expansion. However, the company faced challenges in aligning its recruitment strategies with evolving business goals. To address this, they partnered with Innovex to refine its executive search and hiring process.

Challenges Identified

The client encountered several hurdles in its executive recruitment efforts:

1. Evolving Leadership Needs: The company's business landscape was shifting, which might result in frequent adjustments to leadership roles and competencies.
2. Competitive Talent Market: Attracting top-tier leaders in the healthcare industry requires a strategic approach.
3. Alignment with Business Goals: Leadership hires needed to seamlessly integrate with the client's long-term vision and operational priorities.
4. Need for Flexibility: A rigid hiring strategy would not

accommodate the client's dynamic requirements, and this necessitated an adaptable recruitment process.

Solution Implemented

Innovex adopted a flexible, results-driven approach to executive recruitment, ensuring the client could attract and retain top talent despite shifting priorities.

Strategic Talent Assessment and Role Definition

- Conducted a deep analysis of the client's business goals and leadership requirements.
- Redefined executive roles to align with the company's strategic direction.
- Developed a dynamic recruitment framework that adapted to their evolving needs.

Targeted Executive Search and Engagement

- Leveraged on the job boards to attract potential candidates for application.
- Engaged with passive and active candidates through personalized outreach strategies.
- Used data-driven selection tools to assess leadership capabilities and cultural fit.

Adaptive Recruitment Process

- Implemented a flexible approach that allowed for iterative role refinements and evolving job specifications.
- Ensured continuous collaboration between the leadership team and Innovex to address emerging requirements.
- Maintained agility in hiring timelines while ensuring top-tier talent acquisition.

Seamless Candidate Evaluation and On boarding

- Conducted rigorous multi-stage assessments, that covers competency-based interviews and situational evaluations.
- Provided onboarding support to ensure new leaders integrated smoothly into the corporate culture.

Results Achieved

One of the major results achieved is securing top-tier leadership talent that is aligned with the business objectives. These newly appointed leaders contributed to the client's strategic growth and operational success. The refined recruitment process led to increased executive engagement and long-term retention.

Key Lessons Learned

Innovex's results-driven recruitment approach combines flexibility, strategic alignment with business goals, and proactive engagement to attract top talent. Our structured executive search ensures long-term leadership stability and delivers tangible business outcomes, driving sustained growth and organizational success.

Key Takeaway

Innovex focuses on delivering measurable outcomes by tailoring solutions to enhance leadership efficiency and streamline recruitment processes. Adapting to each organization's unique needs, we provide expert solutions to secure high-skilled leadership talent for critical roles, ensuring your business is equipped with top-tier leaders. Each client is treated as a new project, allowing us to bring fresh ideas and customized solutions for maximum satisfaction. Trust Innovex to maximize your organization's potential—contact us today to elevate your leadership and drive long-term success.

9

Taking Action: Steps, Tools & Templates for Leadership Alignment and Strategic Execution

Effective leadership requires more than just vision; it demands strategic action that aligns personal leadership style with organizational objectives. This section provides a step-by-step guide on how leaders can bridge the gap between strategy and execution using proven tools and templates.

Step 1: Clarify Organizational Goals

Before taking action, the first thing every leader must do is to have a clear understanding of the organization's mission, vision, and strategic objectives. The organizational mission, visions and strategic objectives should be well written down and documented. This ensures that employees can go through it to understand the organization's overarching priorities. To ensure clarity of organizational goals, you need to adopt a structured approach, and one such is SWOT analysis.

A SWOT (Strengths, Weaknesses, Opportunities, and Threats) analysis is a valuable tool that you can adopt to help in the understanding of the internal and external factors that affect an organization. Leaders should:

- Assess Strengths: Identify unique capabilities that give the company an advantage in the industry or areas the company excels in. It can be a strong brand reputation, financial stability, a loyal customer base, or a skilled workforce. For example, a tech company with a robust R&D department can leverage innovation as a competitive edge.
- Identify Weaknesses: This refers to recognizing internal challenges or areas the company needs improvement on, such as outdated technology, inefficient processes, or a lack of skilled personnel. A retail chain struggling with slow inventory turnover can focus on streamlining supply chain operations.
- Explore Opportunities: This entails looking for external potential areas, structures and initiatives that give this company an advantage, such as market expansion, part-nerships, and technological advancements. For instance, an e-commerce company might capitalize on the rise of mobile shopping by optimizing its app and website.
- Recognize Threats: This implies considering external risks such as economic downturns, regulatory changes, or rising competition. A manufacturing firm facing supply chain disruptions can mitigate risks by diversifying its suppliers.

Conducting a comprehensive SWOT analysis helps leaders refine strategic goals and allocate resources effectively. For example, a healthcare startup that identifies limited brand recognition as a weakness will place greater emphasis on investing in a targeted marketing campaign to build awareness and attract customers.

By understanding these factors, leaders can create strategic objectives that are realistic, actionable, and aligned with long-term success. Organizations that regularly perform SWOT analyses can proactively adapt to changing environments and maintain a competitive edge in the industry.

After conducting a SWOT Analysis, the next thing to do to have a precise understanding of the organization's goals is to review the key performance indicators (KPIs). KPIs provide measurable insights into business performance and progress toward strategic objectives. To ensure clarity, leaders should:

- Identify Critical KPIs: Select key metrics that align with organizational success, such as revenue growth, customer retention rates, employee engagement scores, and operational efficiency. For example, a SaaS company might focus on customer churn rates and monthly recurring revenue to gauge stability and growth.
- Ensure Alignment with Organizational Goals: KPIs should be directly linked to strategic objectives. Setting benchmarks and performance standards helps track progress. A manufacturing firm aiming for sustainability might track energy efficiency and waste reduction as key indicators.
- Regularly Review and Adjust KPIs: Market conditions, technological advancements, and internal shifts can affect business goals. As a leader, you must periodically assess KPIs to ensure relevance. A retail chain experiencing shifts

in consumer preferences may need to adjust inventory turnover metrics to reflect new shopping behaviors.

Effective use of KPIs ensures that efforts remain focused on areas that drive long-term success. For instance, a company looking to improve customer satisfaction might measure Net Promoter Score (NPS) and implement changes based on customer feedback.

The last step towards clarifying organizational goals is engaging with stakeholders in dialogue. As a leader, you should:

- Communicate with Key Stakeholders: Engage employees, customers, investors, and partners to gather insights on expectations and concerns. You can align their inputs with the results of the SWOT analysis and KPIs to streamline and identify the most pressing goals that you need to focus on.
- Facilitate Strategic Planning Sessions: Involve various teams in goal-setting processes. For instance, a nonprofit organization might conduct strategy workshops with board members and volunteers to refine its fundraising initiatives.
- Use Stakeholder Feedback to Adjust Priorities: Insights from stakeholders can help refine mission and vision statements. If employees express concerns about work-life balance, leadership can prioritize policies that promote flexibility and well-being.

Step 2: Define Leadership Priorities

Once organizational goals are clear, the next essential step is to determine the most critical actions that will drive success. Effective prioritization enables teams to focus on high-impact activities. Strategies that will help you in defining and ensuring the achievement of the most pressing priority include:

- Setting SMART Goals
- Prioritize High-Impact Activities
- Delegate Responsibilities Strategically

Setting SMART Leadership Goals

SMART (Specific, Measurable, Achievable, Relevant, and Time-bound) goals provide a structured approach to leadership priorities. It entails defining goals in clear and specific terms. For example, instead of setting a vague objective like "improve productivity," you can say, "increase employee productivity by 15% within six months by implementing a performance tracking system and offering skill development workshops."

Next is to establish measurable benchmarks. To track progress, leaders should set clear performance indicators. For instance, if a goal is to enhance customer satisfaction, a measurable benchmark could be increasing the Net Promoter Score (NPS) from 60 to 75 within a year.

Next, you have to ensure the goals are realistic and aligned with available resources. Although, leaders are encouraged to be ambitious and set high goals, you have to ensure that it is

TAKING ACTION: STEPS, TOOLS & TEMPLATES FOR LEADERSHIP...

within the confine of being achievable. A small business aiming to expand internationally within a year might be unrealistic, but setting a goal to enter one new regional market is more feasible.

Next is to focus on relevant initiatives that directly contribute to the business's success. Goals should align with the company's broader mission and vision. If a company prioritizes sustain- ability, a relevant goal could be reducing waste production by 30% through improved recycling programs.

Next is to time bound the goals by setting deadlines to create urgency and accountability. Time-bound goals ensure a sense of urgency and commitment. For example, a sales team may aim to increase revenue by 20% within the next quarter by launching targeted marketing campaigns.

SMART goals help leaders maintain clarity, enhance focus, and drive effective execution, which translates leadership efforts into meaningful business outcomes.

Prioritize High-Impact Activities

The second strategy is to prioritize high-impact tasks. Not all tasks contribute equally to business success, so you must be able to identify activities with the greatest potential to drive growth, efficiency, and competitive advantage. As a leader, you must be able to assess which tasks have the most significant impact on achieving business objectives. For example, improving customer service processes may have a greater long-term impact than minor administrative changes.

Also, you can use prioritization frameworks to identify high-impact tasks. One of the most potential frameworks to adopt is the Eisenhower Matrix. This tool helps categorize tasks into four quadrants based on urgency and importance:

- Quadrant 1: Do (Urgent and Important)
- Quadrant 2: Schedule (Important but Not Urgent)
- Quadrant 3: Delegate (Urgent but Not Important)
- Quadrant 4: Delete (Neither Urgent Nor Important)

Each quadrant helps you decide what action to take—whether it's immediate action, scheduling for later, delegating, or eliminating.

Quadrant 1: Do (Urgent and Important): These tasks require immediate attention as they directly impact operations or long-term success. They're critical with clear consequences if delayed.

- Examples: Handling a customer crisis or addressing a critical system failure.
- Key Insight: Constantly dealing with these tasks can cause burnout. Mitigate by planning and delegating to prevent frequent crises.

Quadrant 2: Schedule (Important but Not Urgent): These refer to strategic activities that support long-term growth without immediate deadlines.

- Examples: Leadership development programs, long-term

marketing strategies, or annual budget planning.

- Key Insight: Neglecting this quadrant hampers future success. Schedule time for strategic planning to ensure consistent progress.

Quadrant 3: Delegate (Urgent but Not Important): These refer to tasks that need quick action but don't significantly impact goals. They can be delegated to others.

- Examples: Scheduling meetings, routine admin work, or low-priority emails.
- Key Insight: Delegate to free up time for high-impact activities. This also develops your team's skills.

Quadrant 4: Delete (Neither Urgent Nor Important): This refers to ow-value activities that distract from meaningful work. They add no real value to the organization.

- Examples: Excessive social media use, irrelevant meetings, or office gossip.
- Key Insight: Minimize or eliminate these tasks to focus on what truly matters. Regularly review your activities to stay productive.

Delegating Responsibilities Effectively

Leadership is not about doing everything alone but empowering teams to execute effectively. After conducting your SMART analysis or your organizational goals and prioritization, the next is to effectively delegate responsibilities to ensure every employee is working strategically toward ensuring the organizational goals. Delegating entails:

1. Assigning Tasks Based on Individual Strengths and Expertise: Leaders should match responsibilities with employees' skills and experience. For example, a marketing manager with expertise in social media should handle digital outreach initiatives, while a data analyst focuses on performance metrics.
2. Providing Clear Instructions and Expectations: Delegation must be accompanied by clear guidelines, including objectives, deadlines, and desired outcomes. For example, suppose you assign a product launch campaign to a team. In that case, you should specify key performance indicators, such as engagement rates and sales conversions, that you use to measure the performance.
3. Monitoring Progress Without Micromanaging: Establish check-in points to review progress while allowing employees autonomy. For instance, as a project manager, you can set bi-weekly status meetings to track milestones rather than interfering with daily tasks.
4. Encouraging Autonomy and Trust to Foster Employee Development: Empowering employees to take ownership of their responsibilities enhances confidence and professional growth. As a leader, you should groom junior team members and allow them to lead a project after the time of grooming to measure their improvement rate and know whether you will trust them with more high-priority tasks.

Delegation maximizes team efficiency, improves productivity, and enables leaders to focus on high-level strategic decision-making. When done effectively, it strengthens organizational capabilities and creates a more engaged workforce.

Step 3: Implement Effective Communication Strategies

Clear and transparent communication is essential for aligning leadership with organizational goals. Without effective communication, misunderstandings can arise, and this can lead to inefficiencies and misalignment. Strong communication ensures seamless collaboration, improves decision-making, and enhances organizational performance. Here are potent ways to implement effective communication strategies:

- Holding Weekly or Bi-Weekly Check-ins: These meetings provide an opportunity to discuss progress, challenges, and upcoming priorities. For example, a marketing team may hold weekly meetings to review campaign performance and adjust strategies accordingly.
- Encouraging Open Discussion: Leaders should create an environment where team members feel comfortable addressing concerns and sharing new ideas. For instance, a brainstorming session can generate innovative solutions for process improvement.
- Using Structured Agendas: A well-planned agenda helps maintain focus and efficiency. Meetings should have clear objectives, time allocations for each topic, and action points to promote and ensure productivity.
- Utilizing Technology for Remote Communication: With remote and hybrid work environments becoming more common, leveraging technology is crucial to maintaining effective communication in such workplace dynamics. You can utilize tools like Slack, Zoom, Microsoft Teams, or

project management platforms such as Asana or Trello to ensure that teams stay connected, no matter where they are located. Encourage consistent use of these tools to streamline communication and ensure information is easily accessible to all team members.

- Fostering Active Listening: Effective communication is a two-way street. As a leader, learn to listen attentively to your subordinates. This helps team members feel heard and understood, which not only improves understanding but also strengthens trust within the team.
- Providing Constructive Feedback: Clear and constructive feedback is key to continuous improvement and alignment. As a leader, focus on giving feedback that is specific, action-able, and supportive, which helps to guide employees on areas to improve while also reinforcing positive behaviors. Regular feedback ensures that the team knows where they stand and what they need to work on.
- Creating Regular Internal Newsletters or Updates: Internal newsletters are a great way to keep all team members informed about important organizational updates, achieve-ments, and upcoming changes. They can provide a platform for leadership to share their vision and strategic direction with the team, ensuring that everyone is on the same page. This also encourages transparency and helps reduce uncertainty within the organization.
- Encouraging Cross-Departmental Communication: Fa-cilitating communication between different departments helps to ensure that everyone is on the same page, espe-cially in organizations with multiple teams working on interconnected projects. Cross-departmental meetings or collaborative tools can help bridge the gap between teams

and birth a more holistic approach to problem-solving and decision-making.

- Clarifying Roles and Responsibilities: Clear communication about each team member's role and responsibilities helps to minimize confusion and overlaps. As a leader, it is your responsibility to ensure that everyone understands their contributions and how they tie into the broader organizational goals. This clarity boosts efficiency and accountability across the organization.
- Promoting Transparency in Decision-Making: Leaders should be transparent in their decision-making processes and ensure that team members understand the reasoning behind major decisions. This helps to build trust and reduces feelings of uncertainty or frustration. Transparent decision-making also helps the team understand their role in the execution of those decisions.

Step 4: Instituting a Culture of Accountability and Continuous Improvement

Accountability is essential for achieving results, while continuous improvement ensures long-term success. As a leader, you must create an environment where employees take responsibility for their actions and strive for ongoing development. When accountability and improvement are embedded into an organization's culture, employees become more engaged, motivated, and committed to achieving collective goals.

To ensure accountability, team members to employees must have a clear expectation of their roles. They can only be accountable for what they understand that is expected of them.

As a leader, you are to:

- Define Job Roles with Specific Deliverables and Performance Metrics: Clearly outlining expectations helps employees know what success looks like in their roles. For example, a customer service representative may be expected to resolve a certain number of inquiries per day while maintaining a high satisfaction rating.
- Communicate Expectations Through Goal-setting and Regular Feedback Sessions: As a leader, meet with employees periodically to discuss goals, provide guidance, and adjust objectives as necessary.
- Ensure Alignment Between Individual and Organizational Objectives: Employees should be able to see how their work contributes to the organization's overall mission. For example, a marketing specialist should understand how their campaigns directly impact sales growth.

You minimize confusion, promote accountability, and enhance performance by setting clear expectations. After ensuring they have a clear understanding of what is expected of them, the next thing to instituting a culture of accountability is to implement a performance review system.

Performance reviews provide valuable insights into individual and team contributions. When the performance review system is well structured, it enhances productivity, engagement, and professional development.

Effective performance management includes:

- Conducting Regular Evaluations to Assess Employee Performance: Annual or quarterly performance assessments allow leaders to track progress and address areas of improvement proactively.
- Providing Constructive Feedback to Encourage Growth and Improvement: Feedback should be specific, actionable, and balanced between strengths and areas that need development. For instance, as a project manager, you highlight an employee's strong organizational skills while recommending ways to improve time management.
- Recognizing and Rewarding Achievements to Boost Motivation: Employees who receive recognition for their contributions are more likely to invest more energy into performing more than the previous times. Leaders can implement rewards such as bonuses, promotions, or public acknowledgment to celebrate outstanding work.

Encouraging Continuous Learning and Development

Ongoing skill development is crucial for organizational growth and to ensure business sustainability. To encourage continuous learning and development, here is what you ought to do as a leader. They are as follows:

- Offer Training Programs, Workshops, and Mentorship Opportunities: Yoo can facilitate employee growth through internal training sessions, external conferences, and mentorship programs.
- Encourage Employees to Pursue Professional Development Through Certifications and Courses: Employees should be supported in advancing their skills through online courses,

industry certifications, and leadership development programs.

- Create a Learning Culture That Values Curiosity, Adaptability, and Innovation: A company that prioritizes continuous learning builds an environment where employees are encouraged to think creatively and seek new solutions. For example, tech companies often support employees in learning emerging programming languages to stay ahead in the industry.

Investing in learning ensures that teams remain competitive, adaptable, and prepared for future challenges. By fostering a culture of accountability and continuous improvement, organizations position themselves for long-term success and sustainable growth.

Step 5: Utilize Tools and Templates for Implementation

To simplify the process of aligning your leadership with organizational goals, some tools and templates will aid you in implementing the strategies. After you have clarified your organizational goals, defined your leadership priorities, and set strategies in place for effective communication and accountability, you need to leverage tools to ensure the seamless execution of your strategies and initiatives.

Here in this section, we will look at tools and templates for implementation you can leverage on:

Strategic Action Plan Template

A Strategic Action Plan serves as a road map for achieving business objectives by breaking down goals into actionable steps. It helps align efforts, allocate resources, and track progress.

How to Utilize:

- Define Your Goals – Establish clear, measurable objectives that align with the organization's vision. Example: "Increase brand awareness by 30% in six months."
- List Key Initiatives – Identify major projects or actions needed to achieve each goal. Example: "Launch a digital marketing campaign, enhance social media presence, and optimize SEO content."
- Assign Responsibilities – Designate accountable individuals or teams for each initiative.
- Set Timelines and Milestones – Establish deadlines to track progress and make necessary adjustments.
- Monitor and Evaluate – Set performance indicators that will be used to assess progress and make data-driven decisions.

Recommended Tools:

- Google Sheets / Microsoft Excel – Create an interactive plan with tracking features.
- Trello / Asana – Manage action plans in a collaborative digital workspace.
- Monday.com – Automate task assignments and progress tracking.

Leadership Development Plan

Developing effective leaders requires a structured approach to skill enhancement and growth opportunities. A Leadership Development Plan ensures continuous improvement and aligns professional growth with organizational needs.

How to Utilize:

- Conduct a Self-Assessment – Identify leadership strengths and areas for growth.
- Set Development Goals – Define short-term and long-term leadership objectives.
- Engage in Training and Mentorship – Enroll in relevant courses, coaching, or mentorship programs.
- Implement Feedback Mechanisms – Regularly seek feedback from peers, employees, and mentors to track progress.
- Track Progress and Adjust Accordingly – Update goals based on new responsibilities and challenges

Recommended Tools:

- 360-Degree Feedback Software (SurveyMonkey, Qualtrics) – Gather comprehensive feedback.
- LinkedIn Learning / Udemy – Access leadership development courses.
- Notion / Evernote – Maintain a leadership journal to document your progress and insights.

OKR (Objectives and Key Results) Tracker

The OKR framework helps you as a leader to align team efforts with overarching business goals by focusing on measurable outcomes.

How to Utilize:

- Define Clear Objectives — Set ambitious but achievable goals. Example: "Improve customer satisfaction by 20% in Q3."
- Establish Key Results — Identify measurable indicators of success. Example: "Reduce customer complaints by 30% and enhance response time by 15%."
- Track Progress Weekly or Monthly — Regularly review OKRs with your team.
- Encourage Transparency — Make OKRs accessible across departments to promote alignment.
- Adapt and Iterate — Adjust OKRs based on performance insights.

Recommended Tools:

- ClickUp / Lattice — Manage and visualize OKRs.
- Google Sheets with KPI Dashboards — Build a custom OKR tracker.
- Weekdone — Automate goal-setting and progress reporting.

Change Management Framework

Implementing organizational changes requires a structured change management framework to ensure smooth transitions and minimize resistance. Here is how you will go about it.

How to Utilize:

- Assess Readiness – Identify potential obstacles to change.
- Develop a Change Roadmap – Outline stages of adoption and key milestones.
- Communicate the Vision – Use storytelling, Q&A sessions, and presentations to align stakeholders.
- Monitor Adaptation – Track engagement, collect feedback, and address concerns proactively.
- Evaluate Impact – Measure success based on performance and adoption rates.

Recommended Tools:

- Prosci ADKAR Model Templates – Structure change initiatives into Awareness, Desire, Knowledge, Ability, and Reinforcement stages.
- Kotter's 8-Step Change Model – Provide a step-by-step guide for managing transitions.
- Miro / Lucidchart – Create visual change management workflows.

Performance Scorecards

Performance Scorecards provide a structured way to track individual and team progress and ensure alignment with strategic goals.

How to Utilize:

- Define Key Metrics – Choose relevant KPIs aligned with business objectives.
- Visualize Data – Use dashboards with graphs and charts for clear interpretation.
- Conduct Regular Performance Reviews – Evaluate employee and team performance quarterly.
- Link Performance to Rewards – Implement incentive structures to boost motivation.
- Encourage Continuous Improvement – Use feedback to drive growth.

Recommended Tools:

- Tableau / Power BI – Build interactive performance dashboards.
- Balanced Scorecard Templates – Use Excel or Google Sheets for tracking.
- Klipfolio / Geckoboard – Automate performance reporting.

Task Delegation Templates

Delegating effectively ensures productivity while preventing burnout. As an effective leader, you must have a potent delegation template you use in assigning roles and responsibilities.

How to Utilize:

- Assess Team Strengths – Assign tasks based on expertise.
- Define Clear Expectations – Specify deliverables and timelines.
- Monitor Progress Without Micromanaging – Use tracking tools to follow up.
- Encourage Autonomy – Allow employees to take ownership of tasks.

Recommended Tools:

- RACI Matrix (Responsible, Accountable, Consulted, Informed) – Clarify decision-making roles.
- Asana / Monday.com – Track delegated tasks in a structured system.

Productivity Enhancement Templates

Time management and workflow optimization are critical for leadership efficiency. Productivity enhancement templates help you streamline operations to ensure effectiveness.

How to Utilize:

- Use the Eisenhower Matrix – Prioritize tasks based on urgency and importance.
- Set SMART Goals – Ensure tasks are Specific, Measurable, Achievable, Relevant, and Time-bound.
- Leverage Automation – Use AI-driven scheduling and task management tools.

Recommended Tools:

- RescueTime / Toggl – Monitor productivity trends.
- Zapier / IFTTT – Automate repetitive tasks.

Step 6: Monitor, Evaluate, and Adjust

Leadership alignment with organizational goals is an ongoing process that requires continuous monitoring, evaluation, and adjustments to ensure long-term success. As organizational environments evolve, you as a leader must be adaptable to keep the strategy aligned with the goals and priorities. This step is crucial to maintaining sustained growth and ensuring that the organization remains on course to achieve its mission.

Here's how leaders can effectively monitor, evaluate, and adjust their approaches:

Conduct Quarterly Strategy Reviews

One of the most effective ways for leaders to ensure alignment with organizational goals is through quarterly strategy reviews. These reviews involve assessing the current strategic objectives, measuring progress, and identifying any changes or shifts that may have occurred within the company or the broader market.

Quarterly reviews allow you to track the performance of the milestones that were set at the beginning of the quarter, ensuring that the company is progressing as planned.

Also, this is the time to assess whether the goals themselves need to be adjusted. Certain objectives are no longer realistic due to unexpected external challenges, such as economic downturns, changes in industry regulations, or shifts in customer demand. By conducting these reviews regularly, you can make any necessary course corrections in a timely manner. This helps ensure that the organization continues to pursue it's most relevant and impactful goals.

Analyze Key Metrics to Measure Effectiveness

Effective monitoring and evaluation depend heavily on identifying and tracking key performance indicators (KPIs). These metrics can provide valuable insight into how well leadership is executing the strategy and if the organization is on track to achieve its objectives. KPIs may include financial performance, employee engagement, customer satisfaction, operational efficiency, or market share growth, depending on the nature of the business.

Analyze these metrics consistently and deeply, seeking not just surface-level data but meaningful patterns that reveal insights about leadership effectiveness. For instance, if a particular department is falling behind in achieving its targets, it may indicate a misalignment between leadership and departmental objectives. Conversely, a surge in customer satisfaction scores could signal that leadership is effectively driving customer-centric initiatives. Analyzing these metrics provides you with tangible data on what is working and what needs attention.

Moreover, a feedback loop is essential. Gather feedback from employees, customers, and stakeholders. This can include surveys, one-on-one meetings, or formal reviews. Gathering input helps you to determine if the alignment they believe exists between the organization's goals and their leadership approach is perceived similarly across different levels of the organization. This external perspective can identify potential blind spots and reveal areas for improvement.

Adapt Leadership Approaches Based on Feedback and Market Trends

In an ever-changing business environment, you must remain flexible and open to adjusting your strategies and leadership styles. Feedback, whether from employees, customers, or market research, can provide valuable insights into how your leadership is perceived and whether it is effectively driving organizational goals. If certain leadership approaches or management styles are found to be ineffective or disengaging, you will be willing to adjust and implement new strategies or leadership behaviors.

Furthermore, always stay informed about broader market trends and industry changes. The external environment often has a direct impact on an organization's ability to achieve its goals. For example, if new technology emerges or competitor strategies shift, you may need to rethink their approach or invest in new capabilities. Regularly analyzing market trends ensures that your leadership is not only in alignment with internal goals but also responsive to external influences that could affect the company's success.

The process of monitoring, evaluating, and adjusting ensures that leadership continues to align with organizational goals, responding to both internal and external challenges as they arise. By staying proactive, flexible, and data-driven, you can build a culture of continuous improvement, driving the organization toward long-term success and sustainability.

Conclusion

- Aligning leadership with organizational goals through deliberate actions is essential for achieving long-term success.
- Utilizing strategic planning ensures that leadership efforts are focused on the right objectives, driving sustainable growth.
- Open and clear communication is vital to ensure that all team members are on the same page and working towards common goals.
- Establishing accountability ensures that leadership remains responsible for achieving goals, fostering a results-driven culture.

Leveraging practical tools and resources helps in executing strategies effectively, driving meaningful impact and growth.

Final Thoughts

Conclusion: The Future of Leadership and Organizational Growth – Empowering You to Lead with Confidence

As we look to the future, it's evident that leadership is evolving. Gone are the days when a simple command-and-control approach defined leadership. As a leader in this current digital and highly competitive business landscape, you must embrace adaptability, emotional intelligence, and a commitment to continuous growth. The future of leadership and organizational growth is not about maintaining the status quo; it is about leading through change, encouraging innovation, and building resilient organizations that can navigate the complexities of a rapidly changing world.

To succeed in this dynamic environment, you must not only guide your teams but also empower them to lead, innovate, and drive the organization toward long-term success. You must invest in continuous growth, both personal and organizational. Leaders are no longer seen solely as decision-makers; they are now regarded as visionaries, motivators, and enablers of change.

The ability to align leadership strategies with organizational goals while also being agile and responsive to shifts in the marketplace has become paramount. However, achieving such alignment requires intentionality, ongoing reflection, and a commitment to monitoring, evaluating, and adjusting leadership approaches based on feedback and emerging trends.

A Next-Step Guide for Leaders:

1. Conduct an Organizational Audit: Evaluate current leadership practices, team dynamics, and organizational culture to identify gaps and areas for improvement.
2. Apply Proven Frameworks: Utilize leadership and management frameworks to enhance strategic alignment, foster innovation, and improve decision-making processes.
3. Implement Retention Strategies: Focus on employee engagement, professional development, and well-being initiatives to retain top talent and cultivate a motivated workforce.
4. Embrace Continuous Learning: Encourage leadership development programs, coaching, and mentorship opportunities to foster a growth mindset at all levels of the organization.
5. Adapt to Emerging Trends: Stay ahead by being proactive in adopting new technologies, sustainability practices, and inclusive leadership models that reflect the evolving business landscape.

FINAL THOUGHTS

Take Action with Innovex

The future of leadership starts with bold, decisive action. Partner with Innovex today to unlock your organization's potential, drive transformational growth, and build a resilient leadership culture equipped to thrive in the face of change.

Contact us via www.innovex.global to schedule a leadership consultation and begin your journey toward sustained success.

References

- PwC. (2016). Family business survey: The challenge of succession planning
- Kotter, J. P. (1996). Leading change. Harvard Business Press
- McKinsey & Company. (2012). The case for talent management: Why talent strategy matters. McKinsey & Company

Books That Have Influenced My Work

- Jim Collins – Good to Great
- Patrick Lencioni – The Five Dysfunctions of a Team
- Daniel Goleman – Emotional Intelligence

Printed in Great Britain
by Amazon